THE BOOK OF JOEL

THE BOOK OF JOEL

A Study Manual

by
MARIANO DI GANGI

BAKER BOOK HOUSE
Grand Rapids, Michigan
Standard Book Number: 8010-2800-0

CONTENTS

I

MEDIUM AND MESSAGE

Our Lord never meant for His Church to be a non-prophet organization. Over the course of the centuries, He has raised up spokesmen to deliver His truth with all integrity. One of these was the prophet Joel. The message he brought was powerful in its time and of abiding relevance to our contemporary situation. We live in a generation concerned over communication. Against the grim possibility of crises erupting into nuclear holocaust, major capitals are linked by "hot line." Great technological advances have been achieved in the medium of mass communication — press, radio, film, television and satelite. Yet we have been less than successful in learning to speak the truth with consistency and compassion to one another as persons and nations.

If we would learn how to speak the truth in love among ourselves, we must first hear what the God above us has to say to the individual, the Church, the world. Through Joel, He causes us to hear a message of stern judgment and redeeming grace. The former is designed to keep us from presumption, the latter to save us from despair.

Who is Joel? His name means "Jehovah is God," and so contains a short confession of faith. Perhaps it points to piety on the part of his father, Pethuel. There were at least twelve others called Joel in the Old Testament, but this man was gifted of God with remarkable insight and foresight.

Joel's prophecy "is one of the briefest and yet one of the most disturbing and heart-searching books" in the Bible. It is "superb extrovert literature, betraying a Judean flavor, but intrinsically concerned with bigger issues than contemporary politics" (Douglas). Joel interprets the events of his day with reference to the nature and purpose of God, and looks ahead in apocalyptic style to the terror and glory of the world to come.

What Joel had to say is as applicable to our century as it was to his particular period of Jewish history. But when did he prophesy? Scholars are of varying opinions regarding the date of Joel's ministry. Some experts place it in the ninth century

B.C., before the rise of Assyria as a threat to Israel. Others hold the view that Joel was active as late as the fourth century B.C. Matthew Henry evaluates the matter with his customary common sense, concluding that "we are altogether uncertain concerning the time when this prophet prophesied."

Considering the date of Joel's ministry as "undecided," and "of no great importance," Calvin focuses on the main themes of the prophecy itself. He writes, "Now the sum of the Book is this: At the *beginning*, he reproves the stupidity of the people, who, when severely smitten by God, did not feel their evils, but on the contrary grew hardened under them.... *Then* he threatens far more grievous evils; as the people became so insensible under all their punishments, that they were not humbled, the Prophet declares that there were evils at hand much worse than those they had hitherto experienced.... *Thirdly,* he exhorts the people to repentance, and shows that there was required no common evidence of repentance; for they had not lightly offended God, but by their perverseness provoked him to bring on them utter ruin: since, then, their obstinacy had been so great, he bids them to come as suppliants with tears, with sackcloth, with mourning, with ashes, that they might obtain mercy; for they were unworthy of being regarded by the Lord, except they thus submissively humbled themselves.... The *fourth* part of the Book is taken up with promises; for he prophesies of the Kingdom of Christ, and shows that now all things seemed full of despair, yet God had not forgotten the covenant he made with the fathers; and that therefore Christ would come to gather the scattered remnants, yea, and to restore to life his people, though now they were lost and dead" (Preface to Joel).

Joel weaves past, present and future into his message. History and eschatology figure prominently in the book that bears his name. Through it all, however, there is no note of speculation. The prophet has a very practical purpose in mind. He would lead us to the experience of grace and the inheritance of glory. May the same Spirit who inspired that prophecy fulfil this purpose in us.

II

THE WORD OF THE LORD (1:1)

Joel's prophecy begins with a statement as sublime as it is simple: "The word of the Lord that came to Joel the son of Pethuel" (Joel 1:1). Here we have a great affirmation about divine revelation. But what is this "word of the Lord"? The phrase points us to oral, personal, and scriptural communication from God.

ORAL

The living God of the Bible speaks to the hearts and minds of men. Idols are both deaf and dumb, but the Lord makes Himself heard, even as He hears the prayers of His people.

He speaks a dynamic, creative word, and the universe comes into being (Gen. 1:3ff.; Ps. 33:6; Heb. 13:3). God is mighty to keep His promises, for He faithfully performs His word (Deut. 9:5; Isa. 55:10ff.).

This God has put His message into the mouths of prophets. As His servants, they have delivered the word to men and nations across the centuries. Isaiah recalls how the Lord confronted him in a temple during a time of national crisis and personal discouragement, and summoned him to go forth as the bearer of His word. The prophet remembers how he confessed his sins of speech in the presence of the holy God, and records the story of the Lord's cleansing grace. That touch of grace prepared him for a prophetic ministry as a servant of the word (Isa. 6:1-8).

Jeremiah repeatedly affirms that the Lord has communicated with him and given him the message to proclaim. He is one of many true prophets "to whom the word of the Lord came" (Jer. 1:2). He declares, "the word of the Lord came unto me" (Jer. 1:4) . . . "the Lord put forth his hand, and touched my mouth. And the Lord said unto me, Behold, I have put my words into thy mouth" (Jer. 1:9).

Prophets prefaced their message often with these words: "Thus saith the Lord." They didn't doubt or debate the possibility of prophecy. They prophesied. And in the course of prophesying or delivering God's message orally, they showed both foresight and insight.

Foresight. Although they were not always aware of the full meaning of the predictions they uttered, since that significance was only disclosed with the actual fulfillment of prophecy, they did speak concerning the future. For example, Isaiah prophesied of the virgin birth and sacrificial death of Christ (7:14; 53:1-12). Zechariah foretold Messiah's trumphal entry into Jerusalem on Palm Sunday, and His betrayal for thirty pieces of silver on the eve of the crucifixion (9:9f.; 11:12f.). Joel heralded the wonderful outpouring of the Holy Spirit in a prophecy of Pentecost (2:28-32).

Insight. The major emphasis of the prophets was to make known the will of God to their contemporaries, so that they would see the true path of conduct and creed to follow. They dealt with the personal and social and theological aspects of sin. They denounced dishonesty in business, corruption in politics, and idolatry in worship. They related eschatology, or the promises and warnings of God for the future, to ethics, or the demands of God for the present.

Consider, for example, the words spoken by one prophet to his generation: "Wash ye, make you clean; put away the evil of your doings from before mine eyes; cease to do evil; Learn to do well; seek judgment, relieve the oppressed, judge the fatherless, plead for the widow. Come now, and let us reason together, saith the Lord: though your sins be as scarlet, they they shall be as white as snow; though they be red like crimson, they shall be as wool. If ye be willing and obedient, ye shall eat the good of the land: But if ye refuse and rebel, ye shall be devoured with the sword: for the mouth of the Lord hath spoken it" (Isa. 1:16-20). This message exposes the hypocrisy of ritual divorced from righteousness, promises great blessings to all who obey God's will, and threatens severe judgments against those who dare to do their own will. You can be sure of the truth of what the prophet says, because "the mouth of the Lord hath spoken it."

In the New Testament, we read of men who succeeded the ancient prophets as spokesmen for God. The apostle Peter referred to the everlasting endurance of the divine word and then identified it with the message he proclaimed: "For ye were as sheep going astray; but are now returned unto the Shepherd and Bishop of your souls" (I Peter 2:25). The apostle Paul

10

thought back to the impact of the gospel on the Thessalonians. When they heard the preaching of Christ, they "received the word of God" spoken by the missionaries — "not as the word of men, but as it is in truth, the word of God" (I Thess. 2:13). When Paul and Barnabas served in Pisidian Antioch, many came "together to hear the word of God" (Acts 13:44). That same word must be heard in faith by us today, if we would find the secret of eternal life.

PERSONAL

The God who sent men His servants the prophets to proclaim His word orally has now spoken to us personally by His Son. As the writer of the letter to the Hebrews puts it, "God, who at sundry times and in divers manners spake in time past unto the fathers by the prophets, Hath in these last days spoken unto us by his Son, whom he hath appointed heir of all things, by whom also he made the worlds; Who being the brightness of his glory, and the express image of his person, and upholding all things by the word of his power, when he had by himself purged our sins, sat down on the right hand of the Majesty on high" (1:1-3).

This same truth is affirmed by the author of the fourth gospel: "In the beginning was the Word, and the Word was with God, and the Word was God" (John 1:1). "... And the Word was made flesh, and dwelt among us, (and we beheld his glory, the glory as of the only begotten of the Father,) full of grace and truth" (John 1:14). "... No man hath seen God at any time; the only begotten Son, which is in the bosom of the Father, he hath declared him" (John 1:18).

Jesus Christ is "the image of the invisible God" (Col. 1:15). He reveals what God is really like. To see Him, is to see the Father. Of course, sin distorts man's vision and perverts his perception. That is why not everyone beholds the truth and grace of God in Jesus Christ. Doubt and unbelief cloud the picture and confuse the sound, so that God's personal Word in His beloved Son does not get through to men. The apostle Paul, after stating his purpose to make the truth of God plain to people, remarks: "But if our gospel be hid, it is hid to them that are lost: In whom the god of this world hath blinded the minds of them which believe not, lest the light of the glorious gospel of Christ, who is the image of God, should shine unto them. For we preach not ourselves, but Christ Jesus the Lord; and ourselves your servants for Jesus' sake. For God, who commanded

11

the light to shine out of darkness, hath shined in our hearts, to give the light of the knowledge of the glory of God in the face of Jesus Christ" (II Cor. 4:3-6).

Jesus Christ is the fulfillment of God's promise to provide a Saviour for the salvation of His people from their sins. When we become aware of this personal Word made flesh, then we realize that Christianity is not merely a matter of accepting certain truths but of trusting a unique Person who is Himself "the truth" (John 14:6). Encountering Him, we are confronted with the need of decision. Neutrality is henceforth impossible. There can only be the response of rejection or faith to this Person of whom the prophets spoke.

"He came unto his own, and his own received him not. But as many as received him, to them gave he power to become the sons of God, even to them that believe on his name: Which were born, not of blood, nor of the will of the flesh, nor of the will of man, but of God" (John 1:11-13).

SCRIPTURAL

We can hear the oral word of God again in our time, and meet the personal Word today, because of the scriptural word. We must depend on that written message for trustworthy knowledge of what the prophets said, and who Jesus Christ is.

In the seventeenth century, the authors of the Westminster Confession of Faith made this classic statement concerning God's written revelation: "Although the light of nature, and the works of creation and providence, do so far manifest the goodness, wisdom, and power of God, as to leave men inexcusable; yet are they not sufficient to give that knowledge of God, and of his will, which is necessary to salvation; therefore it pleased the Lord, at sundry times, and in divers manners, to reveal himself, and to declare that his will unto his church; and afterwards for the better preserving and propagating of the truth, and for the more sure establishment and comfort of the church against the corruption of the flesh, and the malice of Satan and of the world, to commit the same wholly unto writing; which maketh the Holy Scripture to be most necessary; those former ways of God's revealing his will unto his people now being ceased" (1:1).

This high doctrine of Scripture, however, was not invented by the Westminster Assembly of Divines. Listen to our Lord's apostles: "All Scripture is given by inspiration of God, and is profitable for doctrine, for reproof, for correction, for instruction in righteousness: That the man of God may be perfect thoroughly furnished unto all good works" (II Tim. 3:16, 17).

"And we have the prophetic word made more sure. You will do well to pay attention to this as to a lamp shining in a dark place, until the day dawns and the morning star rises in your hearts. First of all you must understand this, that no prophecy of scripture is a matter of one's own interpretation, because no prophecy ever came by the impulse of man, but men moved by the Holy Spirit spoke from God" (II Peter 1:19-21, RSV).

These inspired writings, of course, come to us through men like Micah, Moses, Malachi and Matthew. But the human authors were guided in their choice of theme and form of expression by the Holy Spirit. He is the ultimate Author of Scripture, and that is why it has supreme authority for us as the infallible rule of faith and practice. We understand what to believe and how to live as we hear the Holy Spirit speaking to us in the Scriptures.

It is deadly to divorce the Scriptures and the Spirit. Those who read the Bible without reverent regard for the Spirit who inspired it will see the words of men but fail to hear the word of God. Those who appeal to the Spirit without engaging in the disciplined study of Scripture, however, fall into subjectivism and fanaticism. We must let the Spirit who inspired the Scriptures illumine us as we read them, so that we come to firm faith in Jesus Christ and commit ourselves to live for God's glory (John 20:30f.).

There is a wonderful interrelationship between the Spirit and the Scriptures. Does the Spirit convict men of sin? So does the word of God (John 16:8f.; Heb. 4:12f.). Does the Spirit comfort believers? So do the Scriptures (John 14:16; Rom. 15:4). Does the Spirit point men to Christ? So does the Bible (John 15:26; 5:39). Indeed, the Spirit accomplishes this ministry of conviction, comfort and testimony through the written word. May we have ears of faith to hear what the Holy Spirit is saying to us in the Scriptures.

UNPRECEDENTED DISASTER (1:2-4)

Joel's message begins with these terrifying words: "Hear this, ye old men, and give ear, all ye inhabitants of the land. Hath this been in your days, or even in the days of your fathers? Tell ye your children of it, and let your children tell their children and their children another generation. That which the palmerworms hath left hath the locust eaten; and that which the locust hath left hath the cankerworm eaten, and that which the cankerworm hath left hath the caterpillar eaten" (Joel 1:2-4).

Is this a rhetorical flourish designed to get our attention? Is it the extravagance of a perpetual pessimist who sees nothing but gloom and doom on the horizon of history? Not at all. What we have here is a realistic description and interpretation of an unprecedented disaster.

DESCRIPTION

Joel describes an event unparalleled in previous generations, so far as he is concerned. Whatever catastrophes may have afflicted people in the past, this particular calamity is unique because it is happening to Joel and his contemporaries. We can read statistics as to the incidence of accident and disease in our nation and be shaken for a fleeting moment. But when we ourselves experience brokenness and illness, that is something else. Impersonal statistics are translated into individual suffering. Then the "averages" become personalized in our own pain. Then the trouble becomes different to anybody else's trouble. As the familiar words of the old Spiritual put it, "Nobody knows the trouble I've seen . . . nobody knows but Jesus."

The prophet speaks of successive waves of locusts ravaging the earth. The ancient world dreaded locusts. Recall the plague of locusts in Egypt: "And the Lord said unto Moses, Stretch out thine hand over the land of Egypt, for the locusts, that they may come up upon the land of Egypt, and eat every herb of the land, even all that the hail hath left. And Moses stretched forth his rod over the land of Egypt, and the Lord brought an east wind upon the land all that day, and all that night; and when it was morning, the east wind brought the locusts. And the locusts went up over all the land of Egypt, and rested in all the coasts of Egypt; very grievous were they; before them there were no such locusts as they, neither after them shall be such. For they covered the face of the whole earth, so that the land was darkened; and they did eat every herb of the land, and all the fruit of the trees which the hail had left; and there remained not any green thing in the trees, or in the herbs of the field, through all the land of Egypt" (Ex. 10:12-15). The fearful scourge that lashed Egypt for a few terrible days now wreaks havoc in "the holy land" over a prolonged period of terror.

The Psalmist referred to God's judgment on the heathen in words like these: "He sent divers sort of flies among them, which devoured them; and frogs, which destroyed them. He gave also their increase unto the caterpillar, and their labor unto the locust" (Ps. 78:45, 46). "He spake, and the locusts came, and caterpillars, and that without number, And did eat up all the herbs in their land, and devoured the fruit of their ground" (Ps. 105:34, 35). Now Joel points to the destructive locusts as instruments of the Lord's chastisement on those who profess to be His privileged people.

Joel mentions "the palmerworm ... locust ... cankerworm ... caterpillar." These terms actually indicate four aspects of the same insect: *gazam,* the cutting locust, gnawing away at vine and fig tree; *arbeh,* the swarming locust, multiplying and migrating in huge numbers; *yeleq,* the hopping locust, licking away substance and leaving only refuse; *chasil,* the destroying locust, devouring the crops of the field. These locusts "are the incarnation of hunger. No voracity is like theirs, the voracity of little creatures, whose million separate appetites nothing is too minute to escape" (G. A. Smith).

INTERPRETATION

Obviously, Joel feels that this catastrophe is of great significance. He calls it to the attention of his contemporaries ("ye old men ... all ye inhabitants of the land") and bids it be related to future generations ("tell ye your children ... let your children tell their children"). But why?

We must remember both the goodness and the severity of God. The memory of God's dealings with His people should never be forgotten. The great and mighty wonders wrought by Him are to be shared with posterity. "We will not hide them from their children, showing to the generation to come the

15

praises of the Lord, and his strength, and his wonderful works that he hath done. For he established a testimony in Jacob, and appointed a law in Israel, which he commanded our fathers, that they should make them known to their children; That the generation to come might know them, even the children which should be born; who should arise and declare them to their children: That they might set their hope in God and not forget the works of God, but keep his commandments: And might not be as their fathers, a stubborn and rebellious generation; a generation that set not their heart aright, and whose spirit was not steadfast with God" (Ps. 78:4-8).

The devastation and desolation brought by the plague of locusts does not happen accidentally. It is a manifestation of God's displeasure over the sins of His people, designed to lead the nation to repentance. In later years, another series of invaders will come — Assyrians, Babylonians, Romans. These will oppress the people and lay waste the land. The Lord of history, through catastrophic events, will confront men with an urgent summons to repentance and the alternative of inevitable doom.

It takes spiritual insight to see what is really happening. Do we discern the signs of the times? The crises of our day, the distress of nations, the chaos of communities, not only reveals our sinful estrangement from God and alienation from one another but rewards man's sinfulness. Persistence in disobedience can only result in deeper ruin. The sovereign God is saying, "Repent or perish!" Do we get the message?

DEADLY ANAESTHESIA (1:5-12)

Drunkards, priests, and virgins people the scene described by the prophet in this passage of Scripture. We do well, in our age of affluence, to consider the wasted heritage and desperate plight of Joel's contemporaries. The grim truth is that it *can* happen here!

WASTED HERITAGE

The prophet's palette holds dark colors, and his brush strokes are bold. His expressions leave us with an impression that is nothing less than depressing.

"The new wine ... is cut off" (Joel 1:5). The symbol of joy is gone. In the providence of God, a strong and numerous "nation" has invaded the land. The locusts that plague the people have teeth that cut and gnaw. This enemy has "the cheek teeth of a great lion" (Joel 1:6).

God is concerned over the calamity that has struck the people and made desolate the land. He speaks of "my land" with deep affection (Joel 1:6). He claims Canaan as His own heritage. Yet although the country may be "sacred to God," it is not exempt from chastisement and judgment (Calvin). You cannot sin with impunity. So long as God is holy and righteous, sinners have no immunity from punishment. The only way to flee from the wrath to come is through repentance for sin and faith in the Saviour.

Extreme is the desolation of the land. God's "vine" is ruined, as the locusts attack leaf and branch (Joel 1:7). It is not merely the vineyards that are laid waste, but the people themselves. In a spiritual sense, they are God's vine. Planted by Him in sovereign grace, nurtured by Him in abiding love, yet Israel has failed to bring forth good fruit. In His righteous displeasure, the Lord cries out: "I will take away the hedge thereof, and it shall be eaten up, and break down the wall thereof, and it shall be trodden down: And I will lay it waste: it shall not be pruned, nor digged; but there shall come up briers and thorns: I will also command the clouds that they rain no rain upon it. For the vineyard of the Lord of hosts is the house of Israel, and the men of Judah his pleasant plant: and he looked for judgment, but behold oppression; for righteousness, but behold a cry" (Isa. 5:5-7).

Christ calls us to be faithful branches of the true vine. Only as we are vitally, personally related to Him do we produce the good fruit that gladdens His heart and glorifies God. Apart from Him — even though we may have a superficial "church connection" — we can do nothing (John 15:1-8).

There is a scarcity of food in the blighted land. The priests have neither food for their sustenance nor what they need for sacrifice in the services of worship. "The meat offering and the drink offering is cut off from the house of the Lord; the priests, the Lord's ministers, mourn" (Joel 1:9).

Once the land was blessed with beauty and bounty. The godly looked out over the countryside and said: "Thou visitest the earth, and waterest it: thou greatly enrichest it with the river of God, which is full of water: thou preparest them corn, when thou hast so provided for it. Thou waterest the ridges thereof abundantly: thou settlest the furrows thereof: thou makest it soft with showers: thou blessest the springing thereof. Thou crownest the year with thy goodness; and thy paths drop fatness. They drop upon the pastures of the wilderness: and the little hills rejoice on every side. The pastures are clothed with flocks; the valleys also are covered over with corn; they shout for joy, they also sing" (Ps. 65:9-13).

"The field is wasted, the land mourneth; for the corn is wasted: the new wine is dried up, the oil languisheth" (Joel 1:10). The landscape no longer smiles. Its scars are painful to behold. "The vine is dried up, and the fig tree languisheth; the pomegranate tree, the palm tree also, and the apple tree, even all the trees of the field, are withered: because joy is withered away from the sons of men" (Joel 1:12).

DESPERATE PLIGHT

The greatest problem facing the people, however, is not the desolation of the land. The greatest problem is the insensibility of soul that does not feel God's chastisement and return to Him in broken-hearted repentance. "This 'anaesthesia' is . . . the very summit of evils." How dreadful, "when men feel not their own calamities, or at least understand not that they are inflicted by the hand of God" (Calvin).

Like sleeping "drunkards," the people fail to make any adequate response to the crisis confronting them (Joel 1:5). They simply do not realize what is happening, nor do they discern why. Else, they would earnestly repent and get back to God. The sad fact is that "all sin stupefies the sinner. All sins intoxicate the mind, bribe and pervert the judgment, dull the conscience, blind the soul, and make it insensible to its own ills. All the passions, anger, vain glory, ambition, avarice, and the rest, are a spiritual drunkenness, inebriating the soul, as strong drink does the body" (Pusey).

The people ought to "lament like a virgin girded with sackcloth for the husband of her youth" (Joel 1:8). As the young maiden weeps over the loss of her betrothed, so the people should deplore their loss of God's favor. Espoused to God in a covenant of love and faith, departing from Him through idolatry, deprived of His presence, yet Israel seems not to care. There is no deep sense of emptiness, no cry of contrition, no plea for reconciliation. Why? Because there is no awareness of the fact that sin has separated their souls from God and brought down misery.

"The harvest of the field is perished," yet neither the "husbandmen" nor the "vinedressers" seem concerned (Joel 1:11). They do not cry over the failure of crops, and their failure to cry is the greater calamity. How sensible are *we* to the ways of God? Do we see His chastisements and judgments in the course of history and repent at the demonstration of His displeasure? Or are we numbered among those who go on with "business as usual," discerning not God's call to repentance in the events of our time?

A nineteenth century writer addressed his contemporaries in these relevant words based on our text: "Prevailing sins are often visited with correseponding judgments. The Lord in His righteous dealings withholds those gifts of His Providence which have been abused. He takes from an ungodly people the means of gratifying their lusts, and leads them to repentance by afflictions which are not capriciously ordered, but with exactest wisdom suited to their character. Thus, to check a thoughtless indifference to religion, He sends forth pestilence which strikes down thousands and spreads universal dismay; to restrain from habits of self-indulgence and extravagance, He causes a blight to fall upon the earth, bringing scarceness and want; to put a rein upon the unsatiated pursuit of wealth, He allows a panic on the Exchange..." (Robinson).

In these times of tumult, as riots, revolts, and wars afflict the nations, are we driven to our knees in honest, humble, heartfelt repentance? Do economic pressures and domestic problems cause us to confess our sins and seek God's grace? His promise of pardon and peace still stands. He encourages us to repent with these gospel words: "If my people who are called by my name humble themselves, and pray and seek my face, and turn from their wicked ways, then I will hear from heaven, and will forgive their sin and heal their land" (II Chron. 7:14, RSV).

V

THE HOWLING MINISTERS (1:13-15)

When sin is not taken seriously, superficial gaiety becomes a depressing possibility. But when we are aware of having transgressed God's law, or convicted of failure to conform to His revealed will, then we are reduced to repentance. Only those who know what it means to grieve over sin can understand the Lord's word: "Blessed are they that mourn: for they shall be comforted" (Matt. 5:4).

THE ALTAR

"Gird yourselves, and lament, ye priests: howl, ye ministers of the altar; come, lie all night in sackcloth, ye ministers of my God: for the meat offering and the drink offering is withholden from the house of your God" (Joel 1:13).

So great is the famine in the land, that the meat and drink offerings are no longer available for the religious observances in the temple. Ritual and ceremony cease. This means the virtual suspension of worship. Surely, the priests have cause to gird themselves with the rough sackcloth that is the outward symbol of inward grief. Let those who minister at the altar in God's house also weep, as one laments over the loss of a beloved friend.

In the Church today, we no longer need an altar to offer up sacrifices for sin. On the altar of Calvary, the Lamb of God was sacrificed once and for all to atone for the sins of His people. The sacrifices we now may bring are those of thanksgiving for grace and the offering of a broken, contrite heart (Heb. 13:15f.; Ps. 51:16f.).

Nor do we still need a class of priests to minister as mediators between God and ourselves. According to the gospel, every believer is a priest privileged with freedom of access into the holy presence of God through the way that is Christ (I Peter 2:5, 9; Heb. 4:14-16).

Nevertheless, we benefit from the ministry of men who rightly use their gifts as "apostles ... prophets ... evangelists ... pastors and teachers" (Eph. 4:11). They are provided by the risen and exalted Lord "for the perfecting of the saints" so that all God's people may fulfil "the work of the ministry" (Eph. 4:12). We all have our part to perform so that the body of Christ, the Church, may be edified. So shall we all grow" in the unity of the faith" to maturity in Christ (Eph. 4:13).

THE ASSEMBLY

A stirring exhortation comes to Jerusalem's religious leaders: "Sanctify ye a fast, call a solemn assembly, gather the elders and all the inhabitants of the land into the house of the Lord your God and cry unto the Lord" (Joel 1:14).

The priests of the Lord are asked to do far more than merely appoint a day of mourning and fasting. They are to "sanctify" the observance, hallowing it "with devotion and with acts meet for repentance. For fasting is not accepted by God, unless done in charity and obedience to His commands" (Pusey). The fasting required of us in our time is especially that of abstinence from sin — the denial of self — the crucifixion of the works of the flesh (Gal. 5:16-24).

The solemn assembly mentioned by the prophet involves "the elders and all the inhabitants of the land." Leadership must be given by "the venerable heads of the nation" (Orelli). Are these men held in high respect by the people? Let them lead the way to this solemn gathering of humiliation and sorrow before the presence of the Lord. In times past, the elders had been entrusted with the care of the covenant people (Ex. 3:16; 4:29; Deut. 31:28). They shared in the instruction of the people concerning the passover observance (Ex. 12:3, 21).When Moses was burdened with the problems of administering justice, the hearing of minor cases was delegated to them (Num. 11:16ff.). They helped govern their communities (Deut. 19:12; 22:15; 25:7). Now the elders are summoned to set an example for others to follow. Privilege involves responsibility.

The purpose of this special convocation is set forth plainly by the prophet. All are to appear in "the house of the Lord" so that they may with one voice "cry unto the Lord." Here we discover the very heart of prayer. Sincerely, earnestly, fervently, we are to confess our sins and seek His help in prayer. Else does prayer become a vain repetition in heathen style, or a listless litany whose leaden wings will never reach heaven.

THE ALMIGHTY

Why the solemn assembly in God's house? Why the fasting

and mourning by priests and ministers, elders and people? The cause is made clear by the announcement of impending doom. The judgment sinners deserve is about to descend as the wrath of God flashes forth from heaven against the unrighteousness of men. "Alas for the day! for the day of the Lord is at hand, and as a destruction from the Almighty shall it come" (Joel 1:15).

"The day of the Lord is at hand." Searing drought, devastating locusts, raging fires, invading armies — all these are but preludes to the coming of "the day of the Lord" whose dawning means final judgment. When this day will dawn, we cannot now be sure. But that it will come we dare not doubt, if Scripture is seriously received as our guide.

Ahead "is the great day of judgment upon all ungodly powers, when God, as the almighty ruler of the world, brings down and destroys everything that has exalted itself against Him; thus making the history of the world, through His rule over all creatures in heaven and earth, into a continuous judgment which will conclude at the end of this course of the world with a great and universal act of judgment, then everything that has been brought to eternity by the stream of time unjudged and unadjusted will be judged and adjusted once for all, to bring to an end the whole development of the world in accordance with its divine appointment, and perfect the Kingdom of God by the annihilation of all its foes" (Keil).

We encounter "the Almighty." Judgment proceeds from Him. This is the God who revealed Himself as the Almighty to Abraham when he wondered how an aged couple could beget a promised child, let alone become the parents of a numerous race (Gen. 17:1-6, 16-21; 18:10-14). Again, the Almighty met Jacob when that Patriarch needed assurance of divine blessing (Gen. 35:11). At the end, the Almighty will unveil His invincible power in support of His incorruptible justice. He is "El Shaddai," the One who destroys as well as creates. The day of the Lord shall come, "like might put forth by the Almighty Himself, to destroy His enemies, irresistable, inevitable, unendurable, overwhelming the sinner" (Pusey).

Through faith in Jesus Christ, we have come to know the Almighty as our loving, forgiving, understanding, heavenly Father. We look at the gift of Christ and know that He is for us. His omnipotence is linked to benevolence as He causes all things to work together for good to them that love Him and have answered His gracious call with penitent and obedient trust (Rom. 8:28). If this God be for us, then "who can be against us?" (Rom. 8:31).

VI

OUT OF THE DEPTHS (1:16-20)

The Westminster Shorter Catechism, first published in 1647, defines prayer as follows: "Prayer is an offering up of our desires to God, for things agreeable to his will, in the name of Christ, with confession of our sins and thankful acknowledgment of his mercies" (Q. 98). The supplication that arises out of the depths of genuine need may not always have polished literary form, but it will have the fervor of desire. Prayer is an offering up of our *desires* to God, that He may help us in our predicament.

PREDICAMENT

Joel describes the predicament of his people in graphic terms. The world of nature is scorched by the withering, blistering heat of the burning sun, unrelieved by cool breezes, overshadowing clouds, or refreshing rains.

"The seed is rotten under their clods, the garners are laid desolate, the barns are broken down; for the corn is withered" (Joel 1:17). The seed sown in hope now shrivels up and rots in the earth. Its germinating power has been lost, and its vitality destroyed, by prolonged drought. And drought is the prelude to dreaded dearth. What use is there now for store-houses, since no harvest shall be reaped and gathered into garners? Let the barns fall into disrepair. Who has anything to keep? All lays desolate and goes to ruin, since no one has hope for any harvest in the forseeable future.

"How do the beasts groan! the herds of cattle are perplexed, because they have no pasture; yea, the flocks of sheep are made desolate" (Joel 1:18). The animals suffer too, as heaven chastises men for their sins. The whole creation seems to groan and travail, enduring chastisement for man's sake (Rom. 8:18-22; Gen. 3:17-19). Herds of cattle wander about in their perplexity, wondering where food and water may be found. The flocks of sheep know not where to go in their distress and desolation.

"The fire hath devoured the pastures of the wilderness, and

the flame hath burned all the trees of the field" (Joel 1:19). After the gnawing of the locusts, there has come the searing, scorching heat of the burning sun. The land is stricken with a calamity whose devastating effect appears to be without remedy. "The rivers of water are dried up, and the fire hath devoured the pastures of the wilderness" (Joel 1:20).

All of this affects the public worship of God and the religious life of the nation. How can the people bring a peace offering, or present the firstfruits of their harvest to God when drought and locusts have laid the land waste? "'Is not the meat cut off before our eyes, yea, joy and gladness from the house of our God?'" (Joel 1:16).

There is a scarcity of food, especially of that food "destined for the altar which was eaten in conformity to the ritual, at the great harvest festivals when gratitude and joy filled every heart" (Bewer). The remembrance of the "joy and gladness" of God's house only intensifies the sadness and sorrow now.

The experience of the nation was also that of David the king in a previous generation. Driven into hiding by the rebellion of his son Absalom, kept from the worship of God observed at the temple in Jerusalem, David wept: "As the hart panteth after the water brooks, so panteth my soul after thee, O God. My soul thirsteth for God, for the living God: when shall I come and appear before God? My tears have been my meat day and night, while they continually say unto me, Where is thy God? When I remember these things, I pour out my soul in me: for I had gone with the multitude, I went with them to the house of God, with the voice of joy and praise, with a multitude that kept holyday" (Ps. 42:1-4).

Do you associate the house of God with "joy and gladness"? Do you delight in public worship, and reverently rejoice in His presence? The Psalmist could say, "I was glad when they said unto me, Let us go into the house of the Lord (Ps. 122:1).

In Joel's day, however, joy and gladness are gone from the house of God, since "when the crops are destroyed, neither first-fruits nor thank-offerings can be brought to the sanctuary to be eaten there at joyful meals" (Keil). Surely, the crisis confronting the prophet and his people is one that involves the "spiritual" no less than the "natural" aspects of human existence.

PRAYER

Out of the depths of this predicament comes a plea to the God of heaven. Interceding for the people, the prophet prays:

"O Lord, to thee will I cry: for the fire hath devoured the pastures of the wilderness, and the flame hath burned all the trees of the field. The beasts of the field cry also unto thee: for the rivers of water are dried up, and the fire hath devoured the pastures of the wilderness" (Joel 1:19, 20).

When it appears that there is no way out, then there is only one way left. Out of the depths, let fervent prayer ascend to the Lord. From Him has come the infliction of chastisement. From Him alone can also come the healing of affliction. So Joel "appeals to God by His own Name, the faithful Fulfiller of His promises, Him Who Is, and Who has promised to hear all who call upon Him. Let others call to their idols, if they would, or remain stupid and forgetful; the Prophet would cry unto God, and that earnestly" (Pusey).

Even the beasts of the wild join Joel in crying out to God for help. Their roaring and waiting arise from the depths of distress to the God of creation and providence. If there is anything worse than affliction, it is either to ignore the trouble or to seek relief from the wrong source. The superstitious know not where to turn, but the self-satisfied are unaware of any plight for which salvation must be sought. "Blessed are the poor in spirit: for theirs is the kingdom of heaven. Blessed are they that mourn: for they shall be comforted. . . . Blessed are they which do hunger and thirst after righteousness: for they shall be filled" (Matt. 5:3, 4, 6).

❈   ❈   ❈

"Grant, Almighty God, that as Thou seest us to be surrounded with the infirmity of our flesh, and so held by and overwhelmed with earthly cares, that we can hardly raise our hearts and minds to Thee — grant, that being awaked by Thy Word and daily warnings, we may at length feel our evils, and that we may not only learn by the stripes thou inflictest on us, but also of our own accord, summon ourselves to judgment and examine our hearts, and thus come to Thy presence, being our own judges; so that we may anticipate Thy displeasure, and thus obtain that mercy which Thou hast promised to all, who turning only to Thee, deprecate Thy wrath and also hope for Thy favour, through the name of our Lord Jesus Christ. Amen."
— Calvin

VII

DESOLATE EDEN (2:1-3)

Writing to the Christians of Rome, the apostle Paul referred to "the goodness and severity of God" (Rom. 11:22). Both these attributes of our God are clearly revealed throughout the Bible. Our text tells us of the Lord's severity in coming judgment. It also points to the goodness of Him who warns because He is "not willing that any should perish, but that all should come to repentance" (II Peter 3:9).

SOUND OF DANGER

God's spokesman cries out, "Blow ye the trumpet in Zion, and sound an alarm in my holy mountain: let all the inhabitants of the land tremble" (Joel 2:1a).

The priests are summoned to blow the trumpet. They are to sound the *shophar,* the curved horn of a ram or bull, to warn the people of approaching danger. Such a trumpet blast called the people to arms against the Midianites and the Amalekites in the days of Gideon (Judges 6:34). As soon as the warning was heard, other trumpeters relayed the call to sentinels on distant hills. Thus were the tribes rallied for battle in the valley of Jezreel.

The trumpet blast of which Joel speaks is to be heard in Zion, in God's holy mountain. Even here, where the Lord is enthroned in His sanctuary, the sound of warning must be heard. Let the inhabitants of Jerusalem know that they cannot sin with impunity. They have no guaranteed security against the judgments of God, regardless of their professed religion and ritual practice. They have sinned, and God will judge. Therefore, "let all the inhabitants of the land tremble," rather than trifle with the Almighty. Let everyone confess his guilt before the Lord, and "flee to the mercy of God" (Calvin).

DARKNESS AND GLOOM

The reason for rousing the people from a false sense of security to a posture of penitence is made plain by the prophets: "the day of the Lord cometh . . . it is nigh at hand" (Joel 2:1b).

That awesome day is described as "a day of darkness and of gloominess, a day of clouds and of thick darkness, as the morning spread upon the mountains: a great people and a strong; there hath not been ever the like, neither shall be any more after it, even to the years of many generations. A fire devoureth before them; and behind them a flame burneth: the land is as the garden of Eden before them, and behind them a desolate wilderness; yea, and nothing shall escape them" (Joel 2:2, 3).

Is this a description of what is about to happen in the prophet's own time? Or is it future, prophesying the apocalyptic finale to the drama of history?

A *plague* of locusts will soon sweep over the land like an invading army. That locust swarm will blot out the sun and darken the land, as once happened in Egypt (Ex. 10:15, 22). The bright, cheering light of the sun will be covered by myriads of insects. As swiftly as the sunrise touches the mountain peaks and then fills the valleys with light, so will these invading insects involve a degenerate generation in darkness and doom.

The devastation wrought by these voracious locusts shall leave the land looking as though a brutal army had recklessly scorched the earth. What was once as fertile and beautiful as "the garden of Eden" becomes "a desolate wilderness," as the hungry horde relentlessly advances.

These locusts come in the providence of God. They are "the scourges by which he chastises his own people" (Calvin). They are "but the faint shadow of coming evils . . . the first harbingers of God's successive judgments" (Pusey).

This plague of locusts, therefore, is but a *prelude* to that final judgment when the wrath of God shall be revealed from heaven against all the unrighteousness of men. In the course of history, the Lord of the universe has permitted Assyrians, Babylonians and Romans to chastise Israel for its sins. He has allowed Vandals and Turks to invade lands that professed the Faith but fell far short of faithfulness. But the end is not yet. Ahead is the final, universal judgment: the great and terrible day of the Lord.

Considering the approaching judgment on those who disregard and disobey the holy God, E. B. Pusey wrote "Wealthy, busy, restless, intellectual, degraded London — sender forth of missionaries, but, save in China, the largest heathen city in the world; converter of the isles of the sea, but thyself unconverted; fullest of riches and of misery, of civilization and of savage life, of refinements and debastment; heart, whose impulses are felt in every continent, but thyself diseased and feeble, wilt thou, in this thy day, anticipate by thy conversion the Day of the Lord, or will it come upon thee, 'as hath never been the like'? Shalt thou win thy lost ones to Christ, or be thyself the birthplace or abode of Antichrist?"

God's warnings and threatenings reveal His goodness as well as his severity. He causes the trumpet blast to be heard because He cares. The sound of danger is meant to awaken our conscience, and move us to reverence, honest confession of sin, and a renewed love of obedience.

VIII

DAY OF WRATH (2:4-11)

All amateur theologians who entertain a sentimental rather than Scriptural view of God will be shocked by the revelation of His wrath in the course of history, climaxed by that final judgment on the day of wrath. We need to recover the Biblical truth regarding God. He is made known to us in His Word as holy and loving, pardoning the penitent and punishing the proud.

The dark side of God is portrayed in this portion of Joel's prophecy. The Almighty sends a fearsome plague of locusts upon the people as a sign of His displeasure against their sin, and a means of reducing them to repentance for that sin.

NO ESCAPE

Joel describes the mighty armada of locusts and the alarm caused by that formidable invasion among the people. The locusts have "the appearance of horses" (Joel 2:4), charging relentlessly ahead, bearing their armed riders ever onward on a mission of destruction. They bring swift and devastating judgment with them wherever they go. There is an Arab saying quoted by Pusey which declares: "In the locust, slight as it is, there is the nature of ten of the larger animals — the face of a horse, the eyes of an elephant, the neck of a bull, the horns of a deer, the chest of a lion, the belly of a scorpion, the wings of an eagle, the thighs of a camel, the feet of an ostrich, the tail of a serpent." Oriental exaggeration? Ask those who have suffered from the sweep of desolating locusts, and see how true the picture really is!

Temporal judgments point forward to that final judgment. Surely, it is not insignificant that the supernatural locusts of the end time are also compared to war horses in Revelation 9:7.

The prophet likens the sound of the destructive swarm to "the noise of chariots on the tops of mountains . . . the noise of a flame of fire that devoureth the stubble" (Joel 2:5). Think of the chariots of the ancients, driven over rough mountain roads at a rapid pace. Imagine the swiftly spreading flame of a fire in the fields. Thus does the invading army of locusts move through the land and make a mockery of man's defences. These locusts, "countless in number and boundless in might are the instruments of God. The strongest defences give no security. Where then is safety, save in fleeing from God displeased to God appeased?" (Pusey).

It is no wonder that, confronted with the resistless advance of the voracious adversary, the faces of the people shall "gather blackness" (Joel 2:6). Their hearts will be stricken with "the utmost consternation imaginable" (Henry). This fear will find expression in the terror of their countenances.

Walls and weapons are powerless to stem the dreadful tide of destruction. The locusts "shall run like mighty men; they shall climb the wall like men of war; and they shall march everyone on his ways, and they shall not break their ranks" (Joel 2:7). "When they fall upon the sword, they shall not be wounded" (Joel 2:8). Neither town nor country is spared, as the locusts destroy the produce of the seasons and produce panic in the souls of men (Joel 2:9).

Let us not lose sight of the fact that all this comes in the providence of God. The relentless movement of the locusts reminds us that "the judgments of God hold on their course, each going straight to that person for whom God in the awful wisdom of His justice ordains it. No one judgment or chastisement comes by chance" (Pusey). The sovereign God works all things "after the counsel of his own will" (Eph. 1:11). It is impossible to sin with impunity. Sin must either be punished or pardoned, but it can never be ignored by the holy Lord.

It is instructive to note that the sudden confrontation with judgment is compared to stealth by which a "thief" surprises his victims (Joel 2:10). Of course, God mercifully warns sinners to flee from the wrath to come, and make their peace with Him through repentance and faith while there is time. But they are deaf to His voice, heedless to His warnings. They despise His forbearance and mock His threatenings. That is why the advent of judgment overtakes them "like a thief." This figure of speech is found in the writings of Peter (II Peter 3:10) and of Paul (I Thess. 5:2). It is also prominent in some sayings of our Lord (Matt. 24:43f.; Luke 12:39). God forbid that we should fail to listen and act upon His word of warning while there is still time.

The locust plague is a prelude and type of the coming and final judgment in "the day of the Lord" (Joel 2:11). That day shall be marked by the quaking of the earth and the darkening of the skies. In what sense? Here we have a picture of the whole universe trembling at the revelation of God's wrath against sin. This description is heightened in the prophecies of Christ Himself (Matt. 24:29; Mark 13:24f.; Luke 21:25f.). The striking imagery points ahead to the manifestation of God's displeasure over sin.

One writer remarks, "I have no doubt that dire commotions of war, despotic fury, revolutionary violence, the overthrow of dynasties, the subversion of governments, calamitous divisions in the Church, and political complications leading on to every kind of anarchy and disturbance, are here represented" (Robinson). Yet all these catastrophic trends and events are but percursors of the wrath to come.

NO ESCAPE?

The prophet asks, "the day of the Lord is great and very terrible; and who can abide it?" (Joel 2:11). Another prophet, looking ahead to the revelation of the righteous Lord, puts a similar, searching question: "But who may abide the day of his coming? and who shall stand when he appeareth? for he is like a refiner's fire . . . (Mal. 3:2).

To this question, the gospel gives us an answer bright with hope. There *is* a way of escape from the wrath to come. That "way" is Jesus Christ. At the end, He will draw near to judge the world. But now, He offers the world saving grace.

If we believe that the sinless Christ took our guilt upon Himself and died on the cross to pay the penalty for our sins, then the judgment of God no longer hangs over our heads. Condemnation is cancelled for those who trust in Christ Jesus as their personal Savior (Rom. 8:1).

Reflecting on the certainty of judgment and man's need of refuge in Christ, many medieval poets wrote about the day of wrath. Most famous of all hymns on this theme is the one whose opening phrase in Latin reads *"Dies irae, dies illa,"* ascribed to Thomas of Celano. Based on that magnificent poem are these verses by Walter Scott:

> That day of wrath, that dreadful day,
> When heaven and earth shall pass away,
> What power shall be the sinner's stay?
> How shall he meet that dreadful day?

Oh, on that day, that wrathful day,
When man to judgment wakes from clay,
Be Thou the trembling sinner's stay,
Though heaven and earth shall pass away!

IX

PENANCE OR REPENTANCE? (2:12-14)

The wrath of God will be revealed from heaven against the unrighteousness of men. That dark and dreadful day of doom draws near. Great and terrible judgments are on their way. "Therefore also now, saith the Lord, turn ye even to me with all your heart, and with fasting, and with weeping, and with mourning: And rend your heart, and not your garments, and turn unto the Lord your God: for he is gracious and merciful, slow to anger, and of great kindness, and repenteth him of the evil. Who knoweth if he will return and repent, and leave a blessing behind him; even a meat offering and a drink offering unto the Lord your God?" (Joel 2:12-14).

GOD DESIRES REPENTANCE

Joel puts it very plainly: God desires radical repentance, not superficial penance. True, he mentions "fasting, weeping, and mourning." As sinners aware of our guilt in God's sight, we know that our approach to Him must express honesty and humility. But let us also understand that the Lord looks for far more than external signs of sorrow over sin. His eyes penetrate right through to the heart of reality. He listens for the ring of truth in our profession of repentance.

All the fasting, weeping, and mourning in the world are of no avail unless we are truly repentant before God's presence. We must rend our hearts rather than our garments. While men may be impressed with dramatic gestures, God looks on the heart.

Of course, it is easier to practice a religion that consists merely in externals — in rules and rituals — rather than experience a spiritual change that results in a godly style of living. It is far less painful to abstain from eating meat than to crucify the flesh. "Let any one search himself," remarks Calvin, "and he will find that he labors under this evil — that he would rather rend his garment than his heart."

What God requires and desires of sinners like ourselves is contrition, confession, and conversion.

First, there must be contrition. We remember the story of Judas Iscariot at this point. He was filled with regret over the betrayal of Jesus into the hands of killers. Remorse drove him at last to suicide. His lifeless body hung from a tree and the veil of his flesh was rent asunder. But his heart remained hard, impenitent, unforgiven.

Do we know what it means to be contrite? God desires that sinners sense their guilt and weep within for what their sins have done to defile self, destroy neighbor, and dishonor Christ. When we experience poverty of spirit, we are on the right road to everlasting enrichment from the treasury of divine grace. When we mourn over our sins, we pass through spiritual winter. Then comes the springtime of God's comfort.

The Psalmist could speak of this in a very personal way. He assures us that "The Lord is nigh unto them that are of a broken heart; and saveth such as be of a contrite spirit" (Ps. 34:18). He says, "The sacrifices of God are a broken spirit: a broken and a contrite heart, O God, thou wilt not despise" (Ps. 51:17).

When the Holy Spirit opens the eyes of the soul, so that man looks on the Christ whom his sins have pierced, he is reduced to mourning because of Him (Zech. 12:10). Such Spirit-wrought conviction issues in contrition.

Elizabeth Clephane puts it this way:

> Upon the cross of Jesus,
>   Mine eye at times can see
> The very dying form of One
>   Who suffered there for me.
> And from my stricken heart with tears
>   Two wonders I confess —
> The wonders of redeeming love
>   And my own worthlessness.

Second, there must be confession. In the garden of Eden, when Adam and Eve were questioned about their faithlessness, they sought to evade personal responsibility by excusing themselves and blaming someone else. Evasion and excuse are still the tactics that come naturally to sinners in our time. We blame our heredity, or our environment, but refuse to admit that we have sinned in God's sight. Confronted with the evidence of the law we've broken, we try to mitigate our guilt by referring to extenuating circumstances. As long as we hide our sins, God threatens to expose them and judge us. Only when we expose our sins to the gaze of God does He mercifully hide them and forgive us.

The prodigal son returned to his father with the confession of sin upon his lips. That confession came from a contrite heart (Luke 15:18, 21). The publican in the temple, unlike the self-righteous Pharisee, acknowledged his transgressions and made confession. He smote upon his breast and prayed, "God be merciful to me a sinner" (Luke 18:13).

It is only "if we confess our sins" that we shall hear the word of absolution from the mouth of the Lord (I John 1:9). To deplore the rising tide of lawlessness in the world, to denounce the crimes of violence so prevalent in our time, is not what is here required. God waits for us to confess *our* sins. There is something intensely personal and painful about God's requirement. But nothing else will do.

That is why we must each of us examine himself in the light of God's truth. Then alone shall every man be aware of his sins — sins of omission as well as commission; sins of word, thought, and deed; sins against self, against society, against the sovereign God. Then shall the contrite heart confess its faults before the Lord.

Third, there must be conversion. Joel speaks of returning to God from whom we have departed. It is the greatest tragedy in life that individuals and institutions turn away from the Lord. A stream may plunge down a mountainside away from its source, at a rapid, reckless rate. A glacier's movement, however, is almost imperceptible. Yet both move downward. Thus it is with men, and families, and churches, and nations. Some fall away from God in a series of dramatic departures from Biblical faith and morals. Others slide downward ever so slowly. But all need to get back to God. All must experience conversion.

Through His spokesman, the Lord says: "Turn ye even to me with all your heart . . . turn unto the Lord your God." (Joel 2:12f.).

We cannot overcome God, for He is omnipotent. We cannot outwit Him, for He is omniscient. We cannot bribe Him, for He is the righteous judge. We cannot outlive Him, for He is the everlasting God. But we may and must entreat Him, for He is merciful. Let us turn to the Lord, turn to Him with the whole heart, turn to Him now while there is time. Now is the accepted time, and now is the day of salvation (II Cor. 6:2). Today, if we would be responsive to His voice, we must not harden our hearts but return to the Lord (Ps. 95:7f.).

Genuine conversion affects your whole pattern of living. There's nothing superficial about it. Among the true converts to the gospel of Christ were the Thessalonians. Recalling their remarkable conversion, the apostle Paul wrote of how they "turned to God from idols to serve the living and true God; and to wait for his Son from heaven, whom he raised from the dead, even Jesus, who delivered us from the wrath to come" (I Thess. 1:9f.).

In His providence, God sometimes leads men to repentance by the abundant evidences of His lovingkindness and forbearance (Rom. 2:4). At other times, He humbles pride and draws the penitent to Himself through chastisements and judgments. This was the experience of perceptive souls in Joel's day.

It is good for us to pass through affliction, if the difficulties of life cause us to be honest with God and return from our backslidings. The Lord chastens and disciplines those whom He loves, that they might share the presence of His holiness. "Now no chastening for the present seemeth to be joyous, but grievous: nevertheless afterward it yieldeth the peaceable fruit of righteousness unto them which are exercised thereby" (Heb. 12:11).

God's Spirit, speaking in the Scriptures, is able to make us contrite. Out of contrition comes confession. And confession is related to conversion. In the process, our personality is wounded. "For the word of God is quick, and powerful, and sharper than any two-edged sword, piercing even to the dividing asunder of soul and spirit, and of the joints and marrow, and is a discerner of the thoughts and intents of the heart. Neither is there any creature that is not manifest in his sight: but all things are naked, and opened unto the eyes of him with whom we have to do" (Heb. 4:12, 13).

Such sorrow of soul, such poverty of spirit, is the prelude to the joy of salvation. The Lord who wounds our pride also heals the penitent.

GOD ENCOURAGES REPENTANCE

Undoubtedly, God desires repentance. We must turn back to God. But can we be sure that He will receive us when we return? What is the basis of confidence? On what does the blessed assurance of acceptance rest?

Our confidence rests on God's promises. In the gospel, we hear the clear word of encouragment. Recall these promises from the heart of God:

Come now, and let us reason together, saith the Lord: though your sins be as scarlet, they shall be as white as snow; though they be red like crimson, they shall be as wool (Isa. 1:18).

For thus saith the Lord unto the house of Israel, Seek ye me, and ye shall live (Amos 5:4).

All that the Father giveth me shall come to me; and him that cometh to me I will in no wise cast out (John 6:37).

Charlotte Elliott has expressed the believer's confidence in the Lord's promises through these familiar lines:

> Just as I am — poor, wretched, blind;
> Sight, riches, healings of the mind,
> Yea, all I need, in Thee to find,
> O Lamb of God, I come.
>
> Just as I am — Thou wilt receive,
> Wilt welcome, pardon, cleanse, relieve:
> Because Thy promise I believe,
> O Lamb of God, I come!

Our confidence ultimately rests on the Person who gives us such gospel promises. Joel encourages us to return to God "for he is gracious and merciful, slow to anger, and of great kindness." That is why we can be sure that He will put away the threatened "evil" of judgment for all who sincerely repent (Joel 2:13).

God reveals Himself in the Bible as "The Lord God, merciful and gracious, longsuffering, and abundant in goodness and truth, keeping mercy for thousands, forgiving iniquity and transgression and sin" (Ex. 34:6f.). While He punishes the impenitent in His righteousness, the Lord assures all who repent of the remission of sins. Behind the gospel promises there stands the person of the God of grace. He encourages us to come back to Him.

Like Moses, let us keep our eyes on the Lord who "is longsuffering and of great mercy, forgiving iniquity and transgression" (Num. 14:18). With David, let us focus on "a God full of compassion, and gracious, longsuffering, and plenteous in mercy and truth" (Ps. 86:15; cf. Ps. 103:8; 145:8).

When a godly leader interceded on behalf of a wayward but repentant people, he made his appeal to the Lord who is "ready to pardon, gracious and merciful, slow to anger, and of great kindness" (Neh. 9:17). And the apostle Peter encourages a return to God when he says that "the Lord . . . is longsuffering to us-ward, not willing that any should perish, but that all should come to repentance" (II Peter 3:9).

Our supreme encouragement is found in Jesus Christ. He reveals God's loving concern for the redemption of His people from the penalty and power of sin. Beholding His service and sacrifice, we know that God cares. "For God so loved the world, that he gave his only begotten Son, that whosoever believeth in him should not perish, but have everlasting life" (John 3:16).

The blessed assurance of divine mercy, however, is followed by a word that seems to raise doubts and keep souls in suspense. The prophet asks, "Who knoweth if he will return and repent, and leave a blessing behind him; even a meat offering and a drink offering unto the Lord your God?" (Joel 2:14).

What does this mean? Think back to the story of David's notorious sin with Bathsheba. After the king confessed his moral failure and returned from his spiritual estrangement, he found forgiveness. Nevertheless, the child born of that illicit relationship did not live. Nor did the sword of discord depart from succeeding generations of the royal family. "God has promised forgiveness of sins and of eternal punishment to those who turn to Him with their whole heart. Of this, there can be no doubt. But He has not promised . . . that He will remit the temporal punishment which He has threatened" (E. B. Pusey). Hence the seeming doubt and suspense in Joel's question. We cannot presume that God will always turn away the temporal consequences of our sins.

But we can be sure that confessed sin becomes forgiven sin. We have God's own word for it. "If we confess our sins, he is faithful and just to forgive us our sins, and to cleanse us from all unrighteousness" (I John 1:9).

While alienation from God means misery, reconciliation brings blessing. The particular blessing mentioned in the text by Joel had great significance for his contemporaries. Due to the plague of locusts, scorching drought, destructive fires, and invading armies, there was famine in the land. Food was so scarce that the "meat offering" and "drink offering" in the temple had ceased. But now, after repentance and reconciliation, the people could look forward to the renewal of worship symbolic of fellowship with God.

Matthew Henry notes that "The plentiful enjoyment of God's

ordinances in their power and purity is the most valuable instance of a nation's prosperity and the greatest blessing that can be desired. If God give the blessing of the meat-offering, and the drink-offering, that will bring along with it other blessings, will sanctify them, sweeten them, and secure them."

We have every need to get back to God, and every encouragement to do so. "Seek ye the Lord while he may be found, call ye upon him while he is near: Let the wicked forsake his way, and the unrighteous man his thoughts: and let him return unto the Lord, and he will have mercy upon him; and to our God, for he will abundantly pardon" (Isa. 55:6, 7).

✿   ✿   ✿

"Grant, Almighty God, that as thou seest us so foolish in our vices, and also so ensnared by the gratifications of the flesh, that without being constrained we hardly return to thee — O grant that we may feel the weight of thy wrath, and be so touched with the dread of it, as to return to thee gladly, laying aside every dissimulation, and devote ourselves so entirely to thy service, that it may appear that we have from the heart repented, and that we have not trifled with thee by an empty pretence, but have offered to thee our hearts as a sacrifice, so that we and all our works might be sacred offerings to thee through our whole life, that thy name may be glorified in us through Christ our Lord. Amen."

— John Calvin

X

GATHER THE PEOPLE (2:15-17)

Why do people go to church? Is it to see their friends, hear the choir, or listen to the preacher? The prophet Joel here describes an extraordinary congregation, gathered together to express national and personal sorrow over the sin that has displeased God and brought down judgment.

THE MEETING

"Blow the trumpet in Zion, sanctify a fast, call a solemn assembly:" (Joel 2:15).

Already, the prophet has called for the people to congregate (Joel 1:14; 2:1). Now, however, he summons the nation to a solemn assembly in even greater detail. There is a time for feasting, but the national crisis calls for fasting. Why fasting? Is this practice encouraged to gain merit in the Lord's sight, as though self-denial could earn the favor of the holy God? Not at all. The nation is summoned to fasting as an expression of sorrow for sin under the pressure of Divine chastisements. By this outward sign of humiliation, accompanying the sincere confession of guilt before Jehovah's majestic presence, the people are to acknowledge themselves as deserving the judgment and desirous of mercy.

Who was to attend this observance of fasting and penitential prayer? The prophet leaves no doubt as to the universality of the summons when he says: "Gather the people, sanctify the congregation, assemble the elders, gather the children, and those that suck the breasts: let the bridegroom go forth of his chamber, and the bride out of her closet" (Joel 2:16).

There are to be no exemptions. Young and old, men and women, all are called to sorrow of heart for the sins of the nation. "Even the bridegroom and the bride, who felt least inclined to mourn and weep and who ordinarily were excused from many functions and duties," are urged to share in this demonstration of genuine contrition (Bewer). There is here no plea for the excuse voiced in the gospel story, "I have married a wife, and therefore I cannot come" (Luke 14:20).

THE MOTIVE

Joel encourages and exhorts the priests who are dedicated to the Lord's service in the serious ministry of penitential prayer: "Let the priests, the ministers of the Lord, weep between the porch and the altar, and let them say, Spare thy people, O Lord, and give not thine heritage to reproach, that the heathen should rule over them: wherefore should they say among the people, Where is their God?" (Joel 2:17).

They are to intercede for the people using the words of a solemn litany, as they meet "between the porch and the altar." Their place is "in the inner court, between the porch at the east end of the temple, I Kings 6:3, and the great altar of burnt-offering in front of it, I Kings 8:64, with their faces turned toward the sanctuary" (Bewer). They thus stand "in the middle," as mediators, between the presence of God and the people of Israel (Calvin).

On one occasion, some idolatrous priests here turned their backs on the sanctuary of the Lord and engaged in the worship of the sun (Ezek. 8:16). Here, also, godly Zechariah rebuked the sins of the people in the power of the Spirit and was martyrd (Chron. 24:20f.; Matt. 23:35). But now the priests are to pray in this place on behalf of the nation, with penitential tears.

Joel makes plain the powerful motivation of these priestly prayers. The central request is for the deliverance of the nation: "Spare thy people, O Lord." Through the seasons of sin and chastisement, there continues a covenant relationship. The Lord has chosen, nurtured, disciplined, and defended this people over the centuries. They belong to Him, as those whom He has created and redeemed. Will He now abandon them for ever?

If the main petition is for rescue from the deadly plague of invading and voracious locusts, however, the great motive is the glory of God. His reputation is at stake. What will the heathen say if the Lord forsakes His penitent people? Will not the pagans profane God's holy name and say either that the Lord is too unconcerned to do anything for His people, or too weak to help them in any significant way? The power and goodness of God would thus be called into question and the Lord's honor obscured by the smoke of heathen blasphemy. That is why the priests ask God "not to give up the people of His possession ... to the reproach of being scoffed at by the heathen" (Keil).

Many centuries before, Moses had also experienced this

motivation. Confronted with the threat of God's judgment on a wayward people, he prayed: "Lord, why doth thy wrath wax hot against thy people, which thou hast brought forth out of the land of Egypt with great power, and with a mighty hand? Wherefore should the Egyptians speak, and say, For mischief did he bring them out, to slay them in the mountains, and to consume them from the face of the earth? Turn from thy fierce wrath, and repent of this evil against thy people. Remember Abraham, Isaac, and Israel, thy servants, to whom thou swarest by thine own self, and saidst unto them, I will multiply your seed as the stars of heaven, and all this land that I have spoken of will I give unto your seed, and they shall inherit it for ever" (Ex. 32:11-13).

The Psalmist, moreover, had known the motive power of zeal for the glory of God. Recall his prayers:

As the hart panteth after the water brooks, so panteth my soul after thee, O God.
"My soul thirsteth for God, for the living God: when shall I come and appear before God?
My tears have been my meat day and night, while they continually say unto me, Where is thy God? (Ps. 42:1-3).

O remember not against us former iniquities: let thy tender mercies speedily prevent us; for we are brought very low.
Help us, O God of our salvation, for the glory of thy name: and deliver us, and purge away our sins, for thy name's sake.
Wherefore should the heathen say, Where is their God? (Ps. 79:8-10).

In our prayers, let us remember to be moved by zeal for God's glory. "It is part of true penitence to plead to God to pardon us, not for anything in ourselves (for we have nothing of our own but our sins) but because we are the work of His hands, created in His image, the price of the Blood of Jesus, called by His name" (Pusey).

XI

THE EVERLASTING MERCY (2:18-20)

In his poem, "The Cotter's Saturday Night," Robert Burns describes the devotional life of a Scottish farmer and his family. He lets us hear the father tell his children,

> An' O! be sure to fear the Lord alway,
> An' mind your duty, duly, morn an' night!
> Lest in temptation's path ye gang astray,
> Implore His counsel and assisting might:
> They never sought the Lord in vain that
> sought the Lord aright!

The prophet Joel, in the words of our text, shows us how God hears and answers the prayers of repentant hearts that sincerely seek Him.

BLESSINGS FROM HEAVEN

In answer to the penitential prayers of priests and people, the Lord reveals His everlasting mercy and sends blessings from above. The Lord shows Himself "jealous for his land," and compassionate towards its inhabitants (Joel 2:18). He takes up their cause and acts for their good. In the midst of wrath, He remembers mercy. God "cannot bear to have His land and people treated . . . scornfully by the nations nor the honor of His name defiled" (Bewer).

The tenderness and lovingkindness of the Lord to the penitent and brokenhearted encourages us to hope in His mercy. He does not break the bruised reed, nor does He quench the smoking flax. By the revelation of His grace, God restores what is bruised and causes the smoking flax to blaze again with brightness for His glory.

What blessings does God bestow on His people to assure them of forgivensss? The prophet describes them as realities in the realms of nature and of grace. Among the natural blessings are refreshing rains and abundant harvests. But the greatest gift will be the outpouring of the Spirit in the messianic age.

As a visible token of His pardoning and restoring love, God

sends "corn, and wine, and oil" to satisfy the needs of His people (Joel 2:19). He gives the sunshine and the rain, the richness of the soil and the vitality of the seed, so indispensable to prosperity. No more shall "the heathen" cast "reproach" upon them as ignored or forsaken of the Lord.

Joel "seems here to exhibit to us a law and a course of God's judgments and mercies upon man's sin. He takes away both temporal and spiritual blessings symbolized here by the corn and wine and oil; upon repentance, He restores them" (Pusey).

Hugo of St. Victor, who lived at the time of Abelard and Bernard of Clairvaux, was one of the most influential theologians of the twelfth century. Unlike some ecclesiastics who became very involved in religious and political affairs, he concentrated on a quiet contemplative life distinguished by piety and deep thought. Commenting on the words of Joel, he exclaimed: "Over and against the wasting of the land, he sets its richness; against hunger, fulness; against reproach, unperilled glory; against the cruelty and incursion of enemies, their destruction and putrefaction; against barrenness of fruits and aridity of trees, their fresh shoots and richness; against the hunger of the word and thirst for doctrine, he brings the fountain of life and the Teacher of righteousness; against sadness, joy; against confusion, solace; against death, life; against ashes, a crown" (quoted in Pusey).

FLIGHT TOWARD THE SEA

Has God used the locust plague to chastise the nation? Now that chastisement has accomplished its work by reducing the people to repentance, the Lord will destroy the destroyer. Speaking for God, the prophet declares: "I will remove far off from you the northern army, and will drive him into a land barren and desolate, with his face toward the east sea, and his hinder part toward the utmost sea, and his stink shall come up, and his ill savor shall come up, because he hath done great things" (Joel 2:20).

The invading army of locusts from the north shall be driven away by the winds of the Almighty, first in one direction and then toward another. The devastating swarm shall be pursued by a fierce blast to the parched and desolate land south of Judah into the "east" or Dead Sea. The remnant of that ravaging horde shall be driven to destruction in the "utmost" or Mediterranean Sea. Thus is the destroyer destroyed.

What God does with the locust plague, He does with heathen

46

powers. For a time, in the course of His providence, God may permit them to afflict His people as a chastisement for their sin. The prophet Habakkuk wondered about this. He knew that the iniquity and impiety of Israel deserved punishment from the hand of the Lord. But when the Lord punished the Israelites by means of the aggressive and cruel Chaldeans, the prophet was shocked. How could God do such a thing? Then Habakkuk realized that God had "established them for correction" (Hab. 1:12) and would eventually judge the Chaldeans for their arrogance.

"Thus," as Matthew Henry observes in scanning God's lordship over history, "those whom God employs for the correction of his people come afterwards to be themselves reckoned with; and the rod is thrown into the fire. Nothing shall remain but the ill savour of them." The kingdoms of this world may for a time be the instruments of chastisement to the Church, but in the end hell's gates shall not prevail. When suffering shall have caused the Lord's people to return to Him with penitence and faith, the oppressors of the Church will be vanquished in the final victory of God.

XII

NO MORE FEAR (2:21-27)

After the storm, a calm. After the rain, a rainbow. Times of chastisement and judgment are followed by seasons of renewal in the gracious providence of the Lord.

Joel perceived that penitence would coincide with the cessation of poverty and plague for the people of God. Repentance was the condition of restoration. When the broken-hearted returned to the Lord, they found Him waiting for them. Truly, the God of the gospel is the waiting Father. He welcomes the returning prodigal in His prodigious grace, and restores him to the privileges of sonship.

Let us consider the revelation of God's goodness to His penitent people, and understand that this amazing grace calls for the response of gladness on our part.

REVELATION OF GOODNESS

God promises to "do great things" (Joel 2:21). He will cause "the pastures of the wilderness" to be green with fresh grass, and prosper the fruitfulness of "the fig tree and the vine" (Joel 2:22). Even the "beasts of the field" shall benefit from the revelation of God's goodness (Joel 2:22). As the world of nature suffered on account of man's sin and shared his misery, so shall it reflect man's restoration to blessing by the grace of God. For, "when God is reconciled to his people, his blessing will smile on the brute creation" (Calvin).

This is a prelude to the wonder of the new heavens and the new earth predicted by the apostle (II Peter 3:13). The best is yet to be. "For the creature waits with eager longing for the revealing of the Sons of God; for the creation was subjected to futility, not of its own will but by the will of him who subjected it in hope; because the creation itself will be set free from its bondage to decay and obtain the glorious liberty of the children of God. We know that the whole creation has been groaning in travail together until now" (Rom. 8:19-22, RSV).

In His great goodness, God reverses the ruin involved in the judgments and chastisements of the past. The land no longer mourns (Joel 1:10), and the beasts of the field no longer groan (Joel 1:18). The locust plague is over, and the drought is at an end. The Lord has revealed His lovingkindness in sending His people an abundance of refreshing rain.

What is the significance of the prophet's reference to "the former rain and the latter rain" (Joel 2:23)? The early rains of October and November prepared the land for the sowing of the seed. The later rains in March and April, would help nourish and ripen the growing crops. God's double blessing in spring and autumn gives us an analogy of His ways in the realm of saving grace. First, He reveals His will through the prophets who faithfully bear the word. Then the Word becomes flesh, as God's beloved Son is sent into the world (Heb. 1:1, 2). First, Jesus Christ accomplishes redemption by dying for the sins of His people. Then the Holy Spirit applies redemption by linking us to Christ and causing us to come alive (Matt. 1:21; II Thess. 2:13). First, there is the experience of the new birth. Then there is spiritual development toward the goal of Christian maturity (John 3:3, 5; Phil. 3:12-14). What God begins in grace, He perfects in glory. He gives both "the former rain and the latter rain."

When God restores the land and blesses the people, desolation is turned into prosperity. Then shall the threshing floors be "full of wheat" and the vats shall "overflow with wine and oil" (Joel 2:24). Refreshing rains, in the providence of God, bring abundant harvests.

With these encouraging words, Joel reminds the people "of God's blessing, and declares that God would be so propitious to them as to pour down his grace upon them and act the part of a father and a guardian towards them" (Calvin). Thus saith the Lord, "I will restore to you the years that the locust hath eaten, the cankerworm, and the caterpillar, and the palmerworm, my great army which I sent among you" (Joel 2:25).

The ravages wrought by the locusts over the years shall be repaired by the hand of the Lord. Chastisement ended, ruin gives way to recovery. "Through repentance, all which had been lost by sin, is restored. In itself deadly sin is an irreparable evil. It deprives the soul of grace, of its hope of glory; it forfeits heaven, it merits hell. God, through Christ, restores the sinner, blots out sin, and does away with its eternal consequences. He replaces the sinner where he was before he fell" (Pusey).

This gracious work of restoration, accomplished by the Lord in the soul of man no less than the soil of a desolate land, is

49

declared by God through His servant Ezekiel: "If a wicked man turns away from all his sins which he has committed and keeps all my statutes and does what is lawful and right, he shall surely live; he shall not die. None of the transgressions which he has committed shall be remembered against him; for the righteousness which he has done he shall live. Have I any pleasure in the death of the wicked, says the Lord God, and not rather that he should turn from his way and live?" (Ezek. 18:21-23, RSV).

When God restores men and heals their land, they "shall eat in plenty, and be satisfied" (Joel 2:26). Exposed to the ridicule and reproach of the heathen when their perversity was visited with chastisement, they shall hereafter be spared from shame. The Lord promises, "My people shall never be ashamed" (Joel 2:26). Their security rests on the favor of Him who restores them in His great goodness.

Thus saith the Lord, "And ye shall know that I am in the midst of Israel, and that I am the Lord your God, and none else: and my people shall never be ashamed" (Joel 2:27). By the revelation of goodness, the Lord manifests His presence among the children of Israel. There is a world of fellowship in these expressions: "your God . . . my people." The true and living God claims men and women as His very own, and would be acknowledged by us as our Lord. This is the heart of biblical religion — the experience of a covenant relationship with God (Lev. 26:11f; Ezek. 37:27; John 14:21, 23; II Cor. 6:16; Rev. 21:3).

RESPONSE OF GLADNESS

Our response to the revelation of God's goodness must be gladness. The prophet cries out, "Fear not, O land; be glad and rejoice: for the Lord will do great things. Be not afraid, ye beasts of the field. . . . Be glad then, ye children of Zion, and rejoice in the Lord your God" (Joel 2:21ff.).

Remembering the mercies of the Lord in transforming desolation and restoring abundance, we are deeply moved to jubilant song. God's gracious work of restoration calls forth a lyrical outburst of joy. This joy is not in the refreshing rains or bountiful harvests. It flows not from the enjoyment of things but the experience of God. The children of Zion "rejoice in the Lord."

The man who has personally met God as Saviour expresses sacred joy in words like these: "I will greatly rejoice in the Lord, my soul shall exult in my God; for he has clothed me with the garments of salvation, he has covered me with the robe of righteousness, as a bridegroom decks himself with a garland, and as a bride adorns herself with her jewels. For as the earth brings forth its shoots, and as a garden causes what is sown in it to spring up, so the Lord God will cause righteousness and praise to spring forth before all the nations" (Isa. 61:10, 11, RSV).

When you know Him as your Redeemer, "you shall rejoice in the Lord; in the Holy One of Israel shall you glory" (Isa. 41:16, RSV). "Rejoice in the Lord.... Rejoice in the Lord always; again I will say, Rejoice" (Phil. 3:1; 4:4, RSV).

Sustained by the abundance of good things He provides, as daily we receive our daily bread and the forgiveness of our trespasses, we should be glad and grateful in His presence. Yet we do not always remember to "praise the name of the Lord" (Joel 2:26). Ingratitude, aggravated by a complaining attitude, wounds the heart of God. What is the response of *our* souls to the revelation of God's goodness?

Henry Francis Lyte was an evangelical Anglican who served a pastorate in Ireland during the first part of the nineteenth century. After he had entered upon the ministry, through a personal-crisis, Lyte was driven to the Bible for the secret of salvation. God spoke to him through the Scriptures, and that experience changed his life. Converted to Christ, Lyte went on to a parish in Devonshire and labored there for many years. In addition to such well known hymns as "Jesus, I My Cross Have Taken" and "Abide with Me," he wrote one whose opening verse gives a glad response to God's goodness:

> Praise, my soul, the King of heaven;
>   To His feet thy tribute bring;
> Ransomed, healed, restored, forgiven,
>   Who like me His praise should sing?
>
> Praise Him, praise Him,
>   Praise Him, praise Him,
> Praise the everlasting King!

XIII

GIFT OF THE SPIRIT (2:28-29)

The same Lord who chastises sinners in their pride blesses them in their penitence. Moved with compassion, He remembers mercy in the midst of wrath. As men repent, He removes the destructive locusts that have plagued the land and restrains invading armies. The face of the earth is made beautiful again through refreshing rains. Now the fields are fertile, and there is new joy over the hope of an abundant harvest.

But man does not live "by bread alone." We need the presence and power of God in our lives. Thus, in the words of John Calvin, we pray: "Grant, Almighty God, that since we lack so many aids while in this frail life, and as it is a shadowy life, we cannot pass a moment, except thou dost continually, and at all times supply through thy bounty what is needful. O grant that we may so profit by thy so many benefits, that we may learn to raise our minds upwards, and ever aspire after celestial life, to which by thy gospel thou invitest us so kindly and sweetly every day, that being gathered into thy celestial kingdom, we may enjoy that perfect felicity, which has been obtained for us by the blood of thy Son, our Lord Jesus Christ. Amen" (Prayer, on Joel 2:28).

What we need, God graciously gives. The Lord says, "And it shall come to pass afterward, that I will pour out my Spirit upon all flesh; and your sons and your daughters shall prophesy, your old men shall dream dreams, your young men shall see visions: And also upon the servants and upon the handmaids in those days will I pour out my Spirit." (Joel 2:28, 29).

PROPHETIC PROMISE

Through His servant Joel, God promised that the Spirit would be abundantly poured out in the concluding and climactic era of human history upon the earth. In the past, the Spirit came upon a few individuals for a specific task during fleeting moments (Judges 6:34; I Sam. 16:13). Hereafter, the Spirit would be received by all kinds of persons as an abiding and powerful presence.

There is a striking *universality* in the prophetic promise: "sons ... daughters ... old men ... young men ... servants ... handmaids." Does this mean that everyone on earth will be filled with God's Spirit? The context of Scripture, corroborated by subsequent history and personal experience, tells us that this promise "does not include every individual in the race, but it includes the whole race and individuals throughout it, in every nation, sex, condition, Jew or Gentile, Greek or Barbarian, educated or uneducated, rich or poor, bond or free, male or female" (E. B. Pusey).

There is also a wonderful *unity* in the results of the Spirit's coming. While forward-looking youth sees "visions" and the slumber-loving age dreams "dreams," they all prophesy. Both dreams and visions are "forms of the prophetic revelation of God" (C. F. Keil). Those whom the Spirit enlightens and empowers will alike perceive and proclaim God's truth. The Spirit will give them all "the rare and singular gift of understanding" the meaning of God's saving acts in history (Calvin). Together, they will bear witness to the Lord's redemptive work for the salvation of His people from the penalty and power of sin.

APOSTOLIC FULFILMENT

Eight centuries passed before the prophetic promise found fulfilment. It happened on the feast of Pentecost, in the year of our Lord's crucifixion, resurrection, and ascension.

Crowds of visitors from many parts of the Roman Empire were gathered in Jerusalem for the observance of Pentecost. A group of Christians were also in the city, praying in one place and with one purpose. They expected the descent of power from heaven, so that they could do the Lord's work on earth. Suddenly, there was the sound of wind and the sight of flame. All who prayed in that fellowship were filled with the Holy Spirit — whether young or old, men or women, rich or poor, bond or free. They began to speak as the Spirit led them, and proclaimed the wonderful works of God. Discerning the meaning of Christ's birth, ministry, death, and resurrection, they declared the gospel plainly to those pilgrims who had gathered in Jerusalem for the festival (Acts 2:1-6).

All who heard were amazed, and marvelled, saying to one another, "Behold, are not all these which speak Galileans? And how hear we every man in our own tongue, wherein we were born? Parthians, and Medes, and Elamites, and dwellers in Mesopotamia, and in Judea, and Cappadocia, in Pontus, and

Asia, Phrygia, and Pamphyllia, in Egypt, and in the parts of Libya about Cyrene, and strangers of Rome, Jews and proselytes, Cretes, and Arabians, we do hear them speak in our tongues the wonderful works of God" (Acts 2:7-11).

While everyone was surprised at what was heard, some reacted with scepticism. In their mockery, they accused the enthusiastic disciples of being drunk with "new wine" (Acts 2:13).

To this accusation, the apostle Peter answered boldly in behalf of the Christian fellowship. He denied intoxication, but affirmed inspiration.

Not intoxication. The man who once suppressed his loyalty to Christ because of fear now courageously confessed Him. He categorically denied the absurd charge of drunkenness. If it was improbable that even drunkards should be intoxicated so early in the day, was it not absurd to accuse persons of temperate reputation of being drunk? Their enthusiasm was not at all due to alcohol, but to the influence of the Spirit of God.

Peter's example shows us that "no ridicule should deter Christians from an honest avowal of their opinions, and a defense of the operations of the Holy Spirit" (Albert Barnes, on Acts 2:14).

Not intoxication, but inspiration. Repudiating the false charge of drunkenness against the disciples, Peter went on to declare the true meaning of what had been seen and heard. He made a very positive defense — an apology in the highest sense of the word — as He ascribed the conduct of the Christian community to the personal, powerful presence of the Holy Spirit. In this amazing event at Pentecost, a prophetic promise found fulfilment: "This is that which was spoken by the prophet Joel; And it shall come to pass in the last days, saith God, I will pour out of my Spirit upon all flesh: and your sons and your daughters shall prophesy, and your young men shall see visions, and your old men shall dream dreams: And on my servants and on my handmaidens I will pour out in those days of my Spirit; and they shall prophesy" (Acts 2:16-18).

Joel's prophecy was fulfilled in the effusion of the Spirit. It happened, as predicted, "in the last days." This corresponds to the prophet's "afterwards" (Joel 2:28).

We are now in the concluding, climactic era of human history on earth. These "last days" began to run their course with the first coming of Christ and will end with His second coming. We are living in the last days (II Tim. 3:1; I Cor. 10:11; Heb. 1:1f.; 9:26; I Peter 1:20).

The Spirit has been poured out on "all flesh" (Joel 2:28f). He descended on disciples and apostles, men and women, young and old, bond and free. Thus did God enlighten and empower "the society of the covenant . . . the Church" to serve Him in this present world (Calvin, on Acts 2:18).

Even servants and slaves receive the gift of the Spirit. As the gospel is preached to the poor, so the presence of Christ's prsonal representative fills their lives when they have the openness of faith. Eventually, the Spirit will also descend on Samaritans (Acts 8:14-17), and Gentiles as well (Acts 10:44-48). Long ago, Moses expressed his hope for the universal outpouring of the Spirit in these words: "Would God that all the Lord's people were prophets, and that the Lord would put his spirit upon them!" (Num. 11:29). Now, in the last days, that wish was granted.

The Christian life involves the reception of Christ as He is offered to us in the gospel for our salvation. Apart from the Saviour, there is lostness and spiritual death. The Christian life also involves the experience of Christ's Spirit within our hearts, causing us to turn from sin and follow after righteousness. The believer is designed by God's electing love to be the temple of the Holy Ghost (I Cor. 3:16). The man who is neither indwelt by the Spirit nor instructed by Him cannot honestly claim to be a Christian (Rom. 8:9).

The effusion of the Spirit had wonderful effects. Those men and women in whose lives He became a reality soon began to witness to Christ. They declared the mighty works of God evident in the virgin birth, compassionate ministry, authoritative teaching, sacrificial death, bodily resurrection, and glorious ascension of our Lord. They discerned that Christ Jesus had come into the world to save sinners. They perceived that Christ died for the sins of His people. They understood that God was in Christ reconciling the world unto Himself. They saw that His triumph over death was the pledge of their own victory over the grave. They presented Christ plainly and powerfully, as the Spirit enabled them to "prophesy" on the day of Pentecost (Acts 2:4, 11, 22-36; John 14:16f.; 15:26f.; 16:13f.).

Beyond Pentecost, that same Spirit gave Peter a vision of evangelism among the Gentiles — beginning with the household of Cornelius (Acts 10:9-22). Paul also saw a vision by night of a Macedonian man who called, "Come over into Macedonia, and help us" (Acts 16:9). Moved by what the Spirit had caused him to see, Paul ventured into Europe with the gospel.

While we may not expect dreams and visions for our guidance today, nor presume to be inspired, yet we should not be strangers from the presence and power of the Spirit. He speaks through the Scriptures. Our sense of direction becomes clear when we listen to His voice with open hearts. As He provides direction through the authoritative writings of the Bible, so He bestows the dynamic we need for the living of these days. The Spirit enables us to resist temptation and obey the revealed will of God as we submit to His leading. He gives us compassionate concern for the uncommitted, and courage to witness faithfully to Jesus Christ, our Saviour and Lord.

XIV

NO OTHER WAY (2:30-32)

The God of the Bible comforts the afflicted and afflicts the comfortable. His severity should keep sinners from presumption, and His goodness is meant to spare the penitent from despair. If the danger of divine judgment is real, the reality of merciful deliverance is also undoubted.

DANGER

Here is a prediction of judgment: "And I will show wonders in the heavens and in the earth, blood, and fire, and pillars of smoke. The sun shall be turned into darkness, and the moon into blood, before the great and the terrible day of the Lord come" (Joel 2:30, 31).

The prophet speaks of "wonders in the heavens," such as the sun being turned into darkness and the moon into blood. He refers to "wonders in the earth," like blood, fire, and pillars of smoke. Surely, these are astounding phenomena. But what do they mean?

Calvin comments on these portents as follows: "So great will be the successor of evils, that the whole order of nature will seem to be subverted." ... The revelation of God's wrath will "fill the whole world with anxiety and fear."

Pusey suggests that "these wonders in heaven and earth began in the first Coming and Passion of Christ, grew in the destruction of Jerusalem, but shall be perfectly fulfilled towards the end of the world, before the final Judgment, and the destruction of the Universe."

Did not a star of unusual brightness shine in the sky at the time of Christ's birtth? By the light of that star, the wise men came from the east to worship the new-born King. When the Lord of glory was crucified, did not the sun become darkened at mid-day? Were not rocks rent and graves opened as a violent earthquake shook the land? May not the ascension of the resurrected Christ be understood as a wonder in the heavens?

What Joel describes in figurative language is the prelude to the dawning of "the great and terrible day of the Lord." The prophet points ahead to "the horizon of time and eternity; the last day of time, the beginning of eternity" (Pusey). We see, then, that "the judgments of God upon a sinful world, and the frequent destruction of wicked kingdoms by fire and sword, are prefaces to and presages of the judgment of the world in the last day" (Henry).

Our Lord tells us of this in His prophecies. He warns, "And ye shall hear of wars and rumors of wars: see that ye be not troubled: for all these things must come to pass, but the end is not yet. For nation shall rise against nation, and kingdom against kingdom: and there shall be famines, and pestilences, and earthquakes, in divers places. All these are the beginning of sorrows" (Matt. 24:6-8). "Immediately after the tribulation of those days shall the sun be darkened, and the moon shall not give her light, and the stars shall fall from heaven, and the powers of the heavens shall be shaken" (Matt. 24:29).

Whatever fulfillment these words have found in the destruction of Jerusalem and other judgments through the centuries, the end is not yet. Ahead is "the great and terrible day of the Lord," the final judgment.

Paul writes of revelation of the Lord Jesus "from heaven with his mighty angels, in flaming fire" to punish "them that know not God, and that obey not the gospel of our Lord Jesus Christ." They shall be "punished with everlasting destruction from the presence of the Lord, and from the glory of his power" when He comes to be "glorified in his saints" (II Thess. 1:7ff.).

Peter refers to the promise of Christ's coming and the scepticism of the ungodly. Then he declares, "But the day of the Lord will come as a thief in the night; in the which the heavens shall pass away with a great noise, and the elements shall melt with fervent heat, the earth also and the works that are therein shall be burned up." (II Peter 3:10). Then the apostle adds a very practical note to this prophecy: "Seeing then that all these things shall be dissolved, what manner of persons ought ye to be in all holy conversation and godliness, Looking for and hastening unto the coming of the day of God, wherein the heavens being on fire shall be dissolved, and the elements shall melt with fervent heat?" (II Peter 3:11, 12). Eschatology and ethics are vitally related. "Wherefore, beloved, seeing that ye look for such things, be diligent that ye may be found of him in peace, without spot, and blameless" (II Peter 3:14).

DELIVERANCE

It is sometimes alleged that the God of the New Testament, in contrast to the deity of the Old Testament, is a God of love rather than wrath. But this false antithesis is exposed for what it is in the clear light of Holy Scripture. The God of Abraham, Isaac, and Jacob revealed His lovingkindness no less than His wrath in ancient times. The God whom Jesus makes known is holy and righteous, as well as merciful. "Our God is a consuming fire," and it is still "a fearful thing to fall into the hands of the living God" (Heb. 12:29; 10:31).

The Lord warns us of the wrath to come, that we may seek the one way of escape while there is time. "And it shall come to pass, that whosoever shall call on the name of the Lord shall be delivered: for in mount Zion and in Jerusalem shall be deliverance, as the Lord hath said, and in the remnant whom the Lord shall call" (Joel 2:32).

Our deliverance is related to invocation. To be "saved," we must invoke "the name of the Lord." The way of salvation from the penalty and power of sin is found as we "call upon the name of the Lord."

But what does this mean? Is it enough to quote the Lord's name in order to be saved? Far more is involved than the bare mention of His name. We must call on the Person represented by His name, make our appeal to Him, and depend on Him alone for our salvation. This is but another way of describing faith.

We have here a most remarkable word, "for God declares that the invocation of his name in a despairing condition is a sure port of safety. . . . God possesses power sufficiently great to deliver us, provided only we call on him" (Calvin).

On that memorable day of Pentecost following our Lord's ascension, the apostle Peter invited repentant sinners to call on the name of the Lord and find salvation (Acts 2:21). The apostle Paul declared that all had sinned and fallen short of God's glory (Rom. 3:23); that the wages of sin would be death (Rom. 6:23); and that the same way of salvation was open to both Jews and Gentiles: "For there is no difference between the Jew and the Greek: for the same Lord over all is rich unto all that call upon him. For whosoever shall call upon the name of the Lord shall be saved" (Rom. 10:12, 13).

For centuries, the godly have committed themselves by an act of faith to this saving Lord (Gen. 4:26; 12:8; I Kings 18:24).

"To call on the name of the Lord implies right *faith,* to call upon Him as He is; right *trust* in Him, leaning upon Him; right *devotion,* calling on Him as He has appointed; right *life,* ourselves who call on Him being or becoming by His grace what He wills" (Pusey).

This is the doctrine of the gospel. God promises, "And call upon me in the day of trouble; I will deliver thee, and thou shalt glorify me" (Ps. 50:15).

Aware of my spiritual hunger, I call on Him who is the Bread of Life. Perplexed, I look to Him who is the Wonderful Counsellor. When plagued by weakness, I look to the Mighty God. Surrounded with moral and spiritual darkness, I turn to Him who is the Light of the World. When I acknowledge the error of my ways, I go to Him who is the Way and go back to God. He is my Shepherd, Master, and Friend. He is my Lord and my God. I trust in Him as He is offered to me in the gospel. I put my confidence in Him alone for salvation. I see in Him the One who was wounded for my transgressions and bruised for my iniquities. Believing on this Lord Jesus Christ, I am saved. I experience deliverance from the wrath to come, and enter into a new life of communion with the living God.

Our deliverance is bound up with vocation. If any man calls on the name of the Lord and finds salvation, it is because he belongs to the "remnant whom the Lord shall call" (Joel 2:32). A generation may degenerate. Yet in every generation, the Lord has His remnant of repentant and believing people. They call on Him, in response to His call. The apostle Peter refers to the initiative of God's grace when, after quoting from Joel's prophecy on the day of Pentecost, he says: "Repent, and be baptized every one of you in the name of Jesus Christ for the remission of sins, and ye shall receive the gift of the Holy Ghost. For the promise is unto you, and to your children, and to all that are afar off, even as many as the Lord our God shall call" (Acts 2:38f.).

The relationship between vocation and invocation is expressed in Paul's description of the Corinthian Christians as "the church of God which is at Corinth . . . them that are sanctified in Christ Jesus, *called* to be saints with all that in every place *call* on the name of Jesus Christ our Lord" (I Cor. 1:2).

Our invocation of the Saviour is a response to His vocation of the sinner. In sovereign grace, He summons Abraham from Ur of the Chaldees, Matthew from a tollbooth, and Zaccheus from a sycamore tree. "It is all of grace. God must first call us by His

grace; then we obey His call, and call on Him" (Pusey).
This is the experience of every believer who has reflected on
the wonder of God's grace:

> I sought the Lord, and afterward I knew
> He moved my soul to seek Him, seeking me;
> It was not I that found, O Saviour true;
> No, I was found of Thee.

> Thou didst reach forth Thy hand and mine enfold;
> I walked and sank not on the storm-tossed sea;
> 'Twas not so much that I on Thee took hold,
> As Thou, dear Lord, on me.

> I find, I walk, I love; but O the whole
> Of love is but my answer, Lord, to Thee!
> For Thou went long beforehand with my soul;
> Always Thou lovedst me.

XV

DIVINE DEFENDER (3:1-8)

God's spokesman now develops the grand theme of the restoration of His people. This restoration would be one of His great surprises — "a thing difficult to believe." Why? "When the mass of the people was so mutilated, when their name was obliterated, when all power was abolished, when the worship of God also, together with the temple, was subverted, when there was no more any form of a kingdom, or even of any civil government — who could have thought that God had any concern for a people in such a wretched condition?" (Calvin).

The Judge of the whole world will call the oppressors of His people to account, and prove Himself to be "a sufficient defender" in behalf of the Church. The Lord's deliverance of the Jews from their foes is but "a prelude to that true and real redemption afterwards effected by Christ. . . . God will not be a half Redeemer, but will continue to work until he completes everything necessary for the happy state of his Church, and makes it perfect in every respect" (Calvin).

THE WORLD'S INJUSTICE

In liberating and restoring His people, the Lord executes judgment on the aggressor and oppressor. The deliverance of the former — involves the doom of the latter. Thus the Judge gathers "all nations" and brings them "down into the valley of Jehoshaphat" (Joel 3:2). Now Jehoshaphat was a king of Judah to whom the Lord granted a remarkable victory over the hostile tribes of Ammon and Moab (II Chron. 20:1-30). But the word rendered "Jehoshaphat" also means "Jehovah judges" or Jehovah has judged." In this wide valley, the Lord waits for the nations. He summons them to judgment for their inhumanity. He charges them with cruel injustice.

Here God "will plead with them . . . for my heritage Israel, whom they have scattered among the nations, and parted my land" (Joel 3:2). This pleading has nothing to do with begging. It is rather the "pleading" of a prosecuting attorney who presents evidence against the accused in building up his case for conviction. The Lord is thus both judge and prosecutor. Although the nations have imagined themselves to have attacked, scattered, and plundered Israel, they have actually assailed the Almighty. To strike at God's people is to strike at God himself. In the words of Matthew Henry, God's people "are his demesne, and therefore he has a good action against those that trespass upon them."

This is a tremendous truth. The apostle Paul learned it the hard way. Journeying on the road to Damascus, "breathing out theatenings and slaughter against the *disciples* of the Lord," he was suddenly confronted with the majesty of the risen Christ who asked, "Saul, Saul, why persecutest thou *me?*" (Acts 9:1-4).

The Church is the body of Christ. To persecute the Church is to attack the Head of the body and incur His wrath. Zechariah comforts and encourages the Lord's people with these words, "He who touches you touches the apple of his eye" (2:8, RSV).

In what ways did the nations show cruelty against the covenant people? Joel mentions several terrible crimes committed by the heathen:

They have "scattered" the people in every direction, driving them far from home, and disrupting the life of countless families (3:2).

They have "parted" the Lord's land of promise, as though it were theirs to dispose of as they desired (3:2).

They "cast lots" for God's people, treating them contemptuously as merchandise to be acquired and resold for the gratification of intemperance and lust. They dared barter young boys in exchange for the services of common prostitutes, and traded young girls for the price of a bottle of wine (3:3).

They took God's "silver and gold" away, and used the prized possessions of His people to adorn their pagan palaces and temples" (3:5).

Surely, they were guilty of inhuman cruelty and detestable sacrilege. Is it any wonder that the holy God, zealous for the cause of His people and the vindication of His glory, should call them to account in the valley of judgment? Sooner or later, perhaps in time and certainly in eternity, the oppressors of God's Church shall face the burning furnace of His wrath.

63

THE LORD'S JUSTICE

It is God who acts in sovereign grace and righteousness for the restoration of His people and the judgment of the ungodly. He declares, "I restore the fortunes of Judah and Jerusalem. ... I will gather all the nations and bring them down to the valley of Jehoshaphat, and I will enter into judgment with them there" (Joel 3:1f., RSV).

Why did the prophet stress this in delivering God's message? "He intended that the faithful, though trodden under foot by the nations, should yet have their grief allayed by some consolation, and know that they were not neglected by God; and that though he connived at their evils for a time, he would yet be their defender, and would contend for them as for his own heritage, because they had been so unjustly treated" (Calvin).

Neither nations nor indivduals can sin with impunity. God sees what is done upon the earth. He hears the cry of Abel's blood as it calls for justice against Cain. The Lord of holiness is not indifferent to injustice. Unless there be repentance and pardon, there shall surely be punishment.

God's justice is not merely designed to restrain or reform the transgressor, but to vindicate God's holy character through retribution for sin. The truth of the retributive justice of God, so clearly taught in Scripture, is strangely neglected in our time. Perhaps this is one of the reasons why men have such a shallow view of sin and are little moved by the thought of judgment.

Joel affirms that as the nations treated the covenant people, so they would be treated by God when He reveals His wrath from heaven against their unrighteousness on earth.

In this world, God has provided civil government for the restraint or punishment of evildoers, and the protection of the properties and persons of the law-abiding. For the administration of earthly justice, He has granted the state what is sometimes called "the power of the sword." We should be thankful for the extent to which human justice reflects the Divine intention in our democratic society (Rom. 13:1-7).

However, in the words of Gilbert and Sullivan, magistrates do not always "make the punishment fit the crime." We must realistically recognize that the judicial process may be perverted as judges are bribed, juries tampered with, and witnesses intimidated. Sometimes, trivial offences receive heavy sentences. More often, serious crimes are given penalties which seem far too light. Not so with the judgment of God. He relates the penalty to the offence with perfection.

Have the heathen shown arrogance and violence against God's people? Have they treated them contemptuously and enslaved them? Have they depersonalized them, disrupted their family life, and hindered their worship? God will deal with them accordingly. Let all nations and societies corrupted by the greed that leads to economic exploitation and the pride that results in prejudiced discrimination know that God will judge them with perfect righteousness, here or hereafter. Let the persecutors of the Church read the handwriting on the wall. The Lord cares, and will in due time avenge His martyrs.

The gathering of the nations for judgment in the Lord's presence, as described by Joel, is the prelude to that final gathering for judgment prophesied by Jesus. His words, recorded in Matthew 25:31-46, fill us with godly fear. Our Lord foretells how "the Son of man shall come in his glory," surrounded with "all his holy angels." The exalted Messiah, possessing power and authority, shall then "sit upon the throne of his glory." In His awesome presence "shall be gathered all nations."

That final crisis or separation will see the everlasting division of the sheep from the goats. The royal Judge shall invite those on His "right hand" to experience the blessedness of the Father and inherit the kingdom prepared for them from the foundation of the world. Those on His "left hand," however, shall hear this terrifying sentence: "Depart from me, ye cursed, into everlasting fire prepared for the devil and his angels."

On what basis will that final judgment proceed? Our Lord will judge the nations with reference to the way they have treated Him in the persons of His people. To feed, clothe, heal, encourage the afflicted is to show compassionate concern for Him. To deny them food, clothing, shelter, or comfort in the hour of their need is to aggravate their plight and mistreat the King. To injure the Church is to wound Christ. Jesus says: "Inasmuch as ye have done it unto one of the least of these my brethren, ye have done it unto me. . . . Inasmuch as ye did it not to one of the least of these, ye did it not to me."

All that God has prophesied through His servants shall surely come to pass. Warnings of coming judgment, like promises of dawning glory, shall be realized. We may not know precisely how, or when, until the time of fulfillment arrives. But the fulfilment itself is beyond all shadow of doubt, "for the Lord hath spoken it" (Joel 3:8).

XVI

VALLEY OF DECISION (3:9-17)

With strong words and vivid expressions, using a graphic style and a staccato rhythm, Joel describes the scene in the valley of decision. His disclosure of final judgment is designed to cause the impenitent dread, and to bring the troubled people of God great comfort.

SUMMONS TO JUDGMENT

The Almighty defiantly challenges the nations of the earth to a final confrontation on the field of battle: "Proclaim ye this among the Gentiles; Prepare war, wake up the mighty men, let all the men of war draw near; let them come up" (Joel 3:9). Let the raging heathen get "ready for war by sacrifices and cultic observances" (Bewer).

While prophets in later centuries will call men to turn from the waging of war to the pursuit of peace (Isa. 2:4; Micah 4:3), this spokesman for God issues a stirring call to arms: "Beat your plowshares into swords, and your pruning hooks into spears: let the weak say, I am strong" (Joel 3:10). Even "the weak" are not exempt from service. As feeling becomes fury, men "forge the tools of peaceful agriculture into weapons of war" (Keil). Thus do they move toward "the closing scene of man's rebellion against God" (Pusey).

As pagan powers conspire together, the prophet prays for the descent of the hosts of heaven and the demonstration of their mighty strength (Joel 3:11). The angels of God, strong and swift to do His holy will, shall execute judgment at God's command (Ps. 78:25; Ps. 103:20). It is significant that Paul portrays the return of Christ to resolve the final crisis in similar terms. He encourages troubled believers, pressured and persecuted by the world, to look ahead. The day will dawn "when the Lord Jesus shall be revealed from heaven with his mighty angels, in flaming fire taking vengeance on them that know not God, and that obey not the gospel of our Lord Jesus Christ: Who shall be punished with everlasting destruction from the presence of the Lord, and from the glory of his power; When he shall come to be glorified in his saints, and to be admired in all them that believe [because our testimony among you was believed] in that day" (II Thess. 1:7-10).

In the course of history, God has delivered His people either through direct intervention (as in the defeat of Pharaoh at the Red Sea), or by permitting one pagan nation to destroy the oppressive power of another (as in the victory of the Medes over Belshazzar of Babylon). At the end, the triumph of God will be clear and complete. Let the Church find comfort in this hope and thus be strengthened to endure. For the Scripture declares that "God takes care of the safety of his Church even in its heaviest afflictions, and that he will be the avenger of wrongs, after having for a time tried the patience of his people and chastised their faults. . . . there will be a turn in the state of things" (Calvin).

SENTENCE IN RIGHTEOUSNESS

The prophet's description now passes from the scene of conflict to the court of justice. Again, he summons men to appear before God. The Lord says, "Let the heathen be awakened, and come up to the valley of Jehoshaphat: for there will I sit to judge all the heathen round about" (Joel 3:12).

The Lord is the defender of His people. That is why "the afflictions of the Church shall not go unpunished; for God at the right time will ascend his tribunal, and cause all nations from every part of the earth to assemble and to be judged there" (Calvin).

Enthroned in awesome majesty for the execution of justice, God gives the word: "Put ye in the sickle, for the harvest is ripe; come, get you down; for the press is full, the vats overflow; for their wickedness is great" (Joel 3:13).

"The harvest is ripe" for reaping. Let the angels of God put in the sharp sickle and cut it down swiftly. There is the gospel harvest of grace, in which men are gathered to God and salvation (John 4:35; Matt. 9:35-38). But at the end, there will be the cutting down of the wicked. It is none other than our Lord Jesus Christ who provides an authoritative explanation of the judgment prophesied through Joel. After telling the parable of the wheat and the tares, Christ explains, "He that soweth the good seed is the Son of man; The field is the world; the good seed are the children of the kingdom; but the tares are the children of the wicked one; The enemy that sowed them is the devil; the harvest is the end of the world; and the reapers are the angels. As therefore the tares are gathered and burned in the fire; so shall it be in the end of this world. The Son of man shall send forth his angels, and they shall gather out of his kingdom all things that offend, and them which do iniquity; and shall cast them into a furnace of fire" (Matt. 15:37-42).

The winepress is full. What the winepress is to gathered grapes, the wrath of God is to the accumulated sins of men. There shall be judgment at the last day, for the holy Lord will not permit human perversity perpetually to pollute His creation.

Looking ahead to that revelation of God's righteousness, Isaiah wrote: "Who is this that comes from Edom, in crimsoned garments from Bozrah, he that is glorious in his apparel, marching in the greatness of his strength? 'It is I, announcing vindication, mighty to save.' Why is thy apparel red, and thy garments like his that treads in the wine press? 'I have trodden the wine press alone, and from the peoples no one was with me; I trod them in my anger and trampled them in my wrath; their lifeblood is sprinkled upon my garments, and I have stained all my raiment. For the day of vengeance was in my heart, and my year of redemption has come'" (Isa. 63:1-4, RSV).

The apostle John shares with us his vision of that fearful, final judgment in these words: "Then I looked, and lo, a white cloud, and seated on the cloud one like a son of man, with a golden crown on his head, and a sharp sickle in his hand. And another angel came out of the temple, calling with a loud voice to him who sat upon the cloud, 'Put in your sickle, and reap, for the hour to reap has come, for the harvest of the earth is fully ripe.' So he who sat upon the cloud swung his sickle on the earth, and the earth was reaped. And another angel came out of the temple in heaven, and he too had a sharp sickle. Then another angel came out from the altar, the angel who has power over fire, and he called with a loud voice to him who had the sharp sickle, 'Put in your sickle, and gather the clusters of the vine of the earth, for its grapes are ripe.' So the angel swung his sickle on the earth, and threw it into the great wine press of the wrath of God; and the wine press was trodden outside the city, and blood flowed from the wine press, as high as a horse's bridle, for one thousand six hundred stadia" (Rev. 14:14-20 RSV).

There are "Multitudes, multitudes in the valley of decision: for the day of the Lord is near in the valley of decision" (Joel 3:14). While in this day of opportunity men are challenged to decision for Christ, in that day God's decision about men will be declared. The Lord will plainly make known His irrevocable determination of the case. From that righteous sentence, there can be no appeal. Surely, the coming revelation of His wrath on sin should move men everywhere to repent and seek reconciliation with God through Christ.

At the last judgment, "The sun and the moon shall be darkened, and the stars shall withdraw their shining" (Joel 3:15). As the stars withdraw their splendor, the scene is gruesome. All nature shrinks from the demonstration of the displeasure of God against sin. Yet even this prophecy of wrath is given in mercy, "to shake off the indifference of men, who carelessly hear and despise all threatenings, except the Lord storms their hearts" (Calvin). The stern warnings of the gospel, like its gracious invitations, come from the heart of Him who is "not willing that any should perish, but that all should come to repentance (II Peter 3:9).

SEQUEL OF KNOWLEDGE

While "the Lord shall roar out of Zion, and utter his voice from Jerusalem" so that "the heavens and the earth shall shake," He will also be "the hope of his people, and the strength of the children of Israel" (Joel 3:16). The strong lion of Judah who terrifies the ungodly is none other than the gentle Shepherd of His chosen flock. He ruins those who exalt themselves against Him in pride, but provides a refuge for all who turn to Him in faith.

When God is truly our hope and strength, we come to a personal knowledge of Him. We have His own promise for it: "So shall ye know that I am the Lord your God dwelling in Zion, my holy mountain: then shall Jerusalem be holy, and there shall no strangers pass through her any more" (Joel 3:17).

Incidentally, what the Scripture here says has to do with grace rather than race. The "Zion" and "Jerusalem" mentioned in these verses refer not to the city in Israel known as such, but to "the sanctified and glorified city of the living God, in which the Lord will be eternally united with His redeemed and sanctified, and glorified Church. We are forbidden to think of the earthly Jerusalem or the earthly Mount Zion, not only by the circumstance that the gathering of all the heathen nations takes place in the valley of Jehoshaphat (i.e., in a portion of the valley of the Kidron, which is pure impossibility), but also by the description which follows the glorification of Judah" (Keil). The reference is thus to "the holy city, new Jerusaelm, coming down from God out of heaven" (Rev. 21:3). It includes Jews and Gentiles who have received grace through faith in Christ and together are heirs of an imperishable glory.

There is a two-fold knowledge of God — "the knowledge of faith" which depends on the promises of Scripture as yet unfulfilled, and "the knowledge of experience" which comes from the actual enjoyment of what God offers in His gospel (Calvin). Whom the Lord delivers from the penalty and power of sin, whom He liberates from the hand of death and the devil, God also gives this "knowledge of experience." Do we know Him as our personal Saviour and Lord?

The Bible encourages us to believe that Jesus Christ has already descended into the deep, dark valley of decision. At the cross, bearing the sins of His people, He endured the judgment of God on that terrible burden. If we now trust in Christ, then our sins have already been judged at Calvary and no condemnation awaits us when the last day dawns.

XVII

GRACE AND GLORY (3:18-21)

Joel's prophecy ends with these words: "And it shall come to pass in that day, that the mountains shall drop down new wine, and the hills shall flow with milk, and all the rivers of Judah shall flow with waters, and a fountain shall come forth of the house of the Lord, and shall water the valley of Shittim.

"Egypt shall be a desolation, and Edom shall be a desolate wilderness, for the violence against the children of Judah, because they have shed innocent blood in their land.

"But Judah shall dwell for ever, and Jerusalem from generation to generation.

"For I will cleanse their blood that I have not cleansed: for the Lord dwelleth in Zion" (Joel 3:18-21).

Matthew Henry notes that "these promises . . . have their accomplishment in the kingdom of glory."

ABUNDANCE OF BLESSING

The prophet speaks of "new wine" coming down from the mountain vineyards of the land, and "milk" flowing from the cattle on the hills. He tells of "rivers" that run and a "fountain" that refreshes. Through these figures of speech, Joel reveals the abundance of spiritual blessing that comes from God. "The prophet here declares that God will be so bountiful to his people, that no good things will be wanting to them either in abundance or variety" (Calvin).

Let us take a closer look at this imagery which "describes the fulness of spiritual blessings which God at all times diffuses through the Church" (Pusey). Joel mentions milk and wine. So does the prophet Amos: "Behold, the days come, saith the Lord, that the plowman shall overtake the reaper, and the treader of grapes him that soweth seed; and the mountains shall drop sweet wine, and all the hills shall melt" (Amos 9:13). These words recall the great gospel invitation given through Isaiah "Ho, every one that thirsteth, come ye to the waters, and he that hath no money; come ye, buy, and eat; yea, come, buy wine and milk without money and without price" (Isa. 55:1). Have we tasted the rich, red wine of God's forgiveness and known the gladness His grace brings? Do we nourish our souls on the milk of His Word?

"All the rivers of Judah shall flow with waters, and a fountain shall come forth of the house of the Lord, and shall water the valley of Shittim" (Joel 3:18). The dry valley of Shittim, or the vale of acacias, shall be refreshed by these waters and caused to flourish. Acacia, incidentally, was the wood used for the building of the ark of the Covenant, as well as the table of shewbread, the tabernacle and its pillars, the altar of burnt-offerings, and the incense. Arid areas and parched valleys shall be touched and transformed by the stream that flows from the God of abounding grace.

Ezekiel also prophesies of a refreshing and renewing stream whose waters flow from the sanctuary of the Lord (47:1-12). It has power to turn the barren land into a fruitful garden. The Psalmist thanks God for the gladdening river whose waters cause the city of God to prosper. He says, "There is a river, the streams whereof shall make glad the city of God, the holy place of the tabernacles of the Most High (Ps. 46:4). In the Revelation, the apostle John writes of "a pure river of water of life, clear as crystal, proceeding out of the throne of God and of the Lamb" (22:1).

What is this, but a beautiful representation of the Spirit who flows from the Father and the Son into the barrenness of human personality and brings life from God? Before He comes, there is dust and desolation and death. His presence means new life, abounding with pardon, peace, and power. Our Lord spoke of this to the woman at the well in Samaria, when He told her about "living water" and promised: "Whosoever drinketh of the water that I shall give him shall never thirst; but the water that I shall give him shall be in him a well of water springing up into everlasting life" (John 4:14).

On another memorable occasion, Christ stood in the temple area during a solemn feast and cried out: "If any man thirst, let him come unto me, and drink" (John 7:37). Through faith, anyone may drink of the living water Christ offers. Receiving this blessing, he becomes a blessing to others. For out of him "shall flow rivers of living waters" (John 7:38). This spake Jesus concerning the Holy Spirit, "which they that believe on him should receive" (John 7:39).

In his great hymn on the precious privileges of God's people, John Newton exclaims:

See! the streams of living waters,
   Springing from eternal love,
Well supply thy sons and daughters,
   And all fear of want remove. '
Who can faint while such a river
   Ever flows their thirst to assuage —
Grace, which like the Lord the Giver,
   Never fails from age to age?

PRESENCE OF GOD

In sharp contrast to the joy of God's people is the desolation of those on whom His judgment falls with finality. Joel does not minimize the dark side of the message God has commissioned him to deliver. Plainly, he prophesies the doom of tyrants and terrorists: "Egypt shall be a desolation, and Edom shall be a desolate wilderness, for the violence against the children of Judah, because they have shed innocent blood in their land" (Joel 3:19).

Does this mean that all the descendants of Abraham are guiltless and perfect? Does the prophet say that every Jew shall be saved, while every Egyptian and Edomite everlastingly lost? Let us never forget that salvation is never by race, but always by grace. And judgment is forever according to truth, in keeping with the facts.

The prophetic word of denunciation is thus directed against the Egyptians involved in the powerful oppression that enslaved Israel and murdered its male children. The threat of desolation is hurled at the Edomites who were hostile to the Hebrews and rejoiced over their calamities. We discern in all this something of the way God governs. In His providence, He sometimes permits the ungodly to afflict His erring people so that chastisement may reduce them to humble repentance. Then He punishes the oppressor for the arrogance and violence displayed in the affliction of His people. Surely, "the triumphing of the wicked is short, and the joy of the ungodly for a moment (Job 20:5). "They that hate righteousness shall be desolate" (Ps. 34:21).

In the day of judgment, God will set things straight. History tells us of the downfall and death of dictators. It records the decay of domineering degenerates given to genocide. Yet not all of God's judgments are meted out in the days of our years. Occasionally, truth seems to be on the scaffold and wrong upon the throne. But at the last day, the wrath of God shall be fully and finally revealed against the disbelieving and disobedient who have persecuted His people, hated His law, spurned His gospel, and defied His majesty.

"But Judah shall dwell for ever, and Jerusalem from generation to generation" (Joel 3:20). Earthly Judah and Jerusalem, being part of this sinful world, shall pass away. But the one true people of God, signified by those terms, shall endure. The gates of hell shall not prevail against the Church of Christ. We have His own unfailing promise for it.

God will vindicate His people, who have suffered innocently in being persecuted for the sake of righteousness and the cause of Christ. He will avenge His slaughtered saints and martyrs by punishing their foes, and thus "cleanse their blood" (Joel 3:21). Best of all, He will dwell in the midst of His people.

"The Lord dwelleth in Zion" (Joel 3:21). This tremendous truth is the focal point of biblical revelation. In ancient times, God revealed His presence among the Israelites by the cloud and fiery pillar that accompanied them night and day on the way to the promised land. He showed His glory in the tabernacle and the temple, to assure the penitent of pardon on the completion of sacrifice for sin. In the fulness of time, God visited this planet personally in Jesus Christ. He is "Immanuel, God-with-us" (Isa. 7:14; Matt. 1:23). All who have eyes of faith can perceive the radiance of God's truth and grace gloriously resplendent in Him. To see Him, is to behold the invisible God (John 1:14; II Cor. 4:6; John 14:9). In Christ, God has drawn near to bear our burden, share our sorrow, endure our temptation, and atone for our sin.

"The Lord dwelleth in Zion." He is present in the midst of His people. The apostle Paul refers to this not only when he writes of the abiding presence of Christ in the heart of the individual believer but especially when he speaks of His presence in the fellowship of the Church. Writing to the Ephesians, Paul says that the one true people of God is drawn from both Jewish and Gentile backgrounds. It is established on the firm foundation of the apostles and the prophets — on the truth of God revealed through their messages and Scriptures. God's Church rests on Jesus Christ as its chief and unifying cornerstone. But for what purpose is the Church thus edified? The answer is clearly given: to be "a holy temple in the Lord ... a habitation of God through the Spirit" (Eph. 2:20ff.). As the Holy Spirit dwells in the midst of God's people, the desire of the Lord's heart is fulfilled.

Here, then, is the goal of Joel's prophecy. What the prophet foretells, the apostle sees. John says, "And I saw a new heaven and a new earth: for the first heaven and the first earth are passed away; and the sea is no more. And I saw the holy city, new Jerusalem, coming down out of heaven from God, made ready as a bride adorned for her husband. And I heard a great voice out of the throne saying, Behold, the tabernacle of God is with men, and he shall dwell with them, and they shall be his peoples, and God himself shall be with them, and be their God: and he shall wipe away every tear from their eyes; and death shall be no more; neither shall there be mourning, nor crying, nor pain, any more: the first things are passed away. And he that sitteth on the throne said, Behold, I make all things new. And he saith Write: for these words are faithful and true. And he said unto me, they are come to pass. I am the Alpha and the Omega, the beginning and the end. I will give unto him that is athirst of the fountain of the water of life freely. He that overcometh shall inherit these things; and I will be his God, and he shall be my son (Rev. 21:1-7, RSV).

BIBLIOGRAPHY

Bewer, Julius A., *A Critical and Exegetical Commentary on Obadiah and Joel,* "International Critical Commentary." Charles Scribner's Sons, New York, 1911.

Calvin, John, *Commentaries on the Twelve Minor Prophets.* Calvin Translation Society, Edinburgh, 1843.

Cameron, G. C., *Joel,* "Hasting's Dictionary of the Bible." Charles Scribner's Sons, New York, 1903.

Carson, J. T., *Joel,* "New Bible Commentary." Inter-Varsity Christian Fellowship, Chicago, 1953.

Conley, Robert & Tortoli, Gianni, "Locusts — Teeth of the Wind," *National Geographic,* August, 1969 (Vol. 136, No. 2). Washington, D.C.

Davis, John D., *Joel,* "A Dictionary of the Bible." Westminster Press, Philadelphia, 1911.

Douglas, G. C. M., *Joel,* "Imperial Bible Dictionary." Blackie & Son, London, 1867.

Douglas, J. D., *Joel,* "New Bible Dictionary." Wm. B. Eerdmans Publishing Co., Grand Rapids, 1962.

Frost, S. B. *The Post-Exilic Prophets,* "Twentieth Century Bible Commentary." Harper & Brothers, New York, 1955. Revised edition.

Graybill, J. B., *Joel,* "The Bible Expositor. Holman, Philadelphia, 1960.

------, *Joel,* "Pictorial Bible Dictionary." Zondervan Publishing House, Grand Rapids, 1963.

Henry, Matthew, *An Exposition of the Old and New Testaments.* James Isbet & Co., London, 1886.

Keil, C. F., *The Twelve Minor Prophets.* T. & T. Clark, Edinburgh, 1868.

Kirkpatrick, A. F., *The Doctrine of the Prophets.* Macmillan, London, 1897. Second edition.

Miller, Madeleine, S. & Miller, J. Lane, *Joel,* "Harper's Bible Dictionary." Harper & Brothers, New York, 1958.

Morgan, G. Campbell, *The Analyzed Bible.* Fleming H. Revell, Westwood, N. J., 1944.

Pusey, E. B., *The Minor Prophets.* Walter Smith, London, 1886.

Robertson, James, *Joel,* "International Standard Bible Encyclopaedia." Wm. B. Eerdmans Publishing Co., Grand Rapids, 1939.

Robinson, E. C., *The Divine Oracles of Joel, Habakkuk, and Zephaniah.* Rivingtons, London, 1865.

Schmoller, Otto, *The Book of Joel,* "Lange's Commentary." Zondervan Publishing House, Grand Rapids, 1960.

Smith, George Adam, *The Book of the Twelve Prophets,* "The Expositor's Bible." Harper & Brothers, New York, 1928.

Thompson, J. A., *Joel,* "The Interpreter's Bible." Abingdon Press, New York, 1956.

Van Zeller, Hubert, *The Outspoken Ones: Twelve Prophets of Israel and Juda.* Sheed & Ward, New York, 1955.

Von Orelli, C., *The Twelve Minor Prophets.* T. & T. Clark, Edinburgh, 1893.

Warren, S. L., *Joel*, "Ellicott's Bible Commentary for English Readers." Cassell, London.

Young, B. J. *An Introduction to the Old Testament.* Wm. B. Eerdmans Publishing Co., Grand Rapids, 1958.